FORCE

Eleni Kitra

Discover the stories of 20 remarkable global leaders in 'Force'. These pioneers have been visionary navigators of change, have showcased courage, curiosity, and an unwavering commitment to creating a better world. Their journeys will ignite your inner Force for transformation.

Writer - Eleni Kitra
Book & Cover Design - David Torres Mora

Registered office
7-8 Church St, Wimborne BH21 1JH

Published by One Golden Nugget
ISBN:
978-1-7384382-9-7

Dedication

I dedicate this book to you Greg and Adamantia, my amazing children. Your constant push, unwavering support, and challenges have been my driving force. You inspire me every day, and this book is a testament to the values and dreams I hold dear, which I hope to pass on to you. Thank you for being my strength and for always being there for me.

Gratitude

I don't consider myself a writer in the traditional sense. Rather, I see myself as so meone who thrives on the energy and inspiration I draw from the people around me. This book is a labor born of curiosity, openness, excitement, and respect, and it simply would not have come into being without the incredible individuals who have journeyed alongside me.

To Amadou Diallo, Anousheh Ansari, Aparna Acharekar, Fares Akad, Joe Foster, Kirthiga Reddy, Melina Taprantzi, Nader Bastaki, Nikos Lagousakos, Noha Hefny, Noor Sweid, Ramez Shehadi, Sallyann Della Casa, Sharon Nishi, Sonia Trigueros, Steven Foster, Subhra Das, and Xavi Anglada: each of you has been a vital part of this journey. Your unique perspectives, insights, and support have not just enriched this book, but have also profoundly enriched my life.

A special note of gratitude to the team at One Golden Nugget, Steven, Anna and Greta and particularly to Steven Foster. Steven, your role in seeding the idea for this book was pivotal. Your constant presence, always keeping up with me, made me feel supported in a way that words can hardly express. You have been a beacon of professionalism, enthusiasm, and great encouragement. My heartfelt thanks also go to Elda Choucair, who graciously wrote the foreword for this book. Elda, your words have added an invaluable dimension to this work, encapsulating its essence with eloquence and insight. Your contribution has been a gift, elevating the narrative and profoundly connecting with readers.

And to you, dear readers, who have chosen to pick up this book and give it a place in your lives – your support means everything to me. These stories, woven from our collective experiences and insights, are now as much yours as they are ours. In this journey of sharing and learning, every conversation, every shared moment, and every nugget of wisdom has been a stepping stone towards the completion of this work. This book is more than just a collection of words; it's a mosaic of thoughts, dreams, and experiences, beautifully unified by our shared human experience. Thank you, from the bottom of my heart, for being a part of this journey.

Contents

Introduction 1

Elda Choucair (Foreword) 2

Amadou Diallo 5

Anousheh Ansari 15

Aparna Acharekar 25

Fares Akad 35

Joe Foster 45

Kirthiga Reddy 53

Melina Taprantzi 65

Nader Al Bastaki 73

Nikos Lagousakos 83

Noha Hefny 89

Noor Sweid 101

Ramez Shehadi 109

Sallyann Della Casa 121

Sharon Nishi 129

Sonia Trigueros 139

Steven Foster 147

Subhra Das 155

Xavi Anglada 161

Eleni Kitra (My Story) 171

Author Bio 181

Introduction

This book is like a conversation with dear friends in my living room, where friends come together to exchange stories that reveal more than just events, but the essence of their experiences.

To me, it is like a collection of life's mosaic, built together by those extraordinary individuals who didn't merely walk on the well-known paths but carved new ones. My lifelong curiosity, always nudging me to peek around life's corners and delve into the unknown, has guided me to these narratives. They are stories of people who didn't just nudge the boundaries of convention but vaulted over them with grace and courage.

These stories are far from the typical hero's journey. They're about everyday people, each with a spark of the extraordinary, who dared to embrace their uniqueness. They're the real life trailblazers who, with resilience and heart, showed us that true change begins within.

Writing this book was crucial for me. It was about bringing together these authentic examples of human courage and spirit to share with you. It was important for me to write this book because it's a tribute to the dreamers, the thinkers, and the doers who've felt their ideas were too grand, too ambitious, or simply too different.

Paraphrasing my mother's saying "It's not about what you can do. It's about what you want to do".

I am saying "Success isn't defined by our abilities but by our aspirations".

And this book is a reminder to all that the journey of a thousand miles begins with a step, and sometimes, that step is believing in the possibility of 'more.'

It's a celebration of human potential, a testament to the power of belief, and a call to embrace the extraordinary within each of us.

ELDA CHOUCAIR

CEO at Omnicom Media Group (MENA)

FOREWORD

In the grand fabric of life, there are threads of connection that weave through our days, connecting us to countless souls who leave a lasting mark on our journey. These connections, these moments of inspiration, are the stuff of which our lives are made. They are the sparks that ignite our passions, the gentle pushes that help us leap over hurdles, and the silent nods of encouragement that tell us we are on the right path. In the pages of this book, you will read the stories behind the one story I will present in this forward so you understand the motivation and essence of this book, the one of Eleni.

Eleni is a woman, whose life began against a backdrop of conservative and traditional values, found herself enveloped in a world that consistently whispered in her ear about her limits, about what she could not do. As life unfolded, she gradually uncovered her true self, one layer at a time. In her success, she came to realize that her story was not hers alone. It was a story shared by many, both men and women, who had also felt the weight of expectations and the discouragement of naysayers.

Force is a remarkable collection of interviews that delve into the hearts and minds of those who influenced the life of its author, a woman whose relentless pursuit of personal growth and self-realization was born from her ability to see the extraordinary in the ordinary. Each conversation, represents a moment of inspiration that Eleni wanted to share with you hoping that it will give you the power you need to push through and be happy.

Throughout these pages, you will meet a diverse cast of characters, each possessing a unique spark, an exceptional quality, or a life-changing moment that ignited a fire within our author. These interviews are a testament to the profound impact that individuals, ordinary and extraordinary, can have on our lives. They remind us that inspiration is all around us, hiding in the corners of everyday encounters, waiting to be discovered by those with open hearts and open minds.

This book is a love letter to the everyday heroes who, knowingly or unknowingly, inspire. It is a testament to the transformative power of relationships and shared experiences. It is a powerful reminder that inspiration, often found in the unlikeliest of places, has the potential to shape our lives in unimaginable ways. As you turn the pages of this book, may you find yourself reflecting on the people who have touched your own life and the threads of inspiration that have woven through your own unique journey. May you be inspired to seek out and celebrate the remarkable individuals who have, in their own way, pushed you to become the best version of yourself.

AMADOU DIALLO

CEO MEA - DHL Global Forwarding

The Change Maker

I first met Amadou back in 2020, during my live interviews for Capital Club's Mobility Series. His ability to effortlessly steer a conversation away from business and into personal territory was immediately captivating. Having the privilege to speak with Amadou means being introduced to new and profound personal reflections, whilst also enjoying the infectious laughter, fascinating debate and emotional bond that he naturally forges.

> "As a little kid, you get used to being underestimated - you can take it either as a sign of disrespect or an opportunity to impress."

As CEO of DHL for the Middle East and Africa, Amadou Diallo's current life is a far cry from the cow herding, nomadic lifestyle of his Fulani heritage. Yet he remains close to his Senegalese roots and attributes a lot of his core beliefs, philanthropic activities, and success to those formative experiences. Like most Muslim boys at the age of four, Amadou Diallo was expected to learn the verses of the Quran by heart, a practice that has resulted in his ability to quickly absorb and retain large amounts of information. Then, at the relatively young age of 15, his father handed him Das Kapital by Karl Marx, a read that sparked his inquisitive teenage mind and set him on a lifelong journey of activism.

By the age of 16, Amadou was already organising strikes and holding rallies to support workers' rights. He was deeply passionate about social equity and improving lives for the majority, but it wasn't until much later that he could look back and reflect on just how much these experiences shaped his identity and approach to business. The memory retention, public speaking, and persuasion skills he developed during his earlier years in Senegal are now what he leans on the most in his leadership roles.

Unfair Advantage

Amadou has never forgotten where he came from. In fact, he considers his "underprivileged background" the very reason for his success. Seeing the injustices around him drove him to learn and create a better world while remaining authentic to his upbringing. He has little time for those who make excuses for their failures, lack of motivation, or inability to pursue more. Switching the narrative, he believes that his humble beginnings actually gave him an "unfair advantage", through an "opportunity to impress." For Amadou it's all about how you reframe things in your mind - what could have been seen as an impossibility due to where he came from became a challenge that he was determined to conquer.

He was even able to rethink to reconsider the social, political, and religious tensions in Senegal as an opportunity to become "a bit more cultivated." As a minority rights activist who wanted to support the small Christian community in Senegal, he decided to read the Bible. It's this hunger for knowledge and ability to embrace opportunity that has afforded him that "unfair advantage".

His focus on reaching his full potential and not letting circumstances prevent him from achieving is something he has passed down to his four children. He teaches them that nothing is out of reach; work harder and learn everything you can so that nothing can stand in your way. If you are ever underestimated, make it your "unfair advantage" and your "opportunity to impress".

The Perpetual Immigrant

As a Fula, Amadou has great empathy for the plights of immigrant communities across the world. He's deeply proud of the strength and resilience of his own immigrant heritage, so much so that he wears the word "immigrant" emblazoned on his t-shirt to show solidarity with those who continue to be "underestimated". A nomad at heart, Amadou remembers his global travels beginning in the UK during the politically charged era of the 1980s, where he was "smuggling whiskey into Ronnie Scotts."

After a few years in the UK, Amadou graduated fluent in English, German, French, Spanish, Fulani and Wolof. This rare skill-set opened a door for him to become CFO of the Logistics Division at Deutsche Post, at only 26 years of age.

Not one to be intimidated, his unique perspective and inquisitive spirit caused him to challenge a lot of people in the organisation. This bold approach caught the eye of EDB Singapore, who invited him to regularly sit with the CEO and discuss all manner of topics.

Eager to experience everything the world had to offer him, Amadou accepted a position as a Board Member for a government agency responsible for the planning and execution of economic strategies in Singapore. This proved to be a pivotal moment as he began to learn how countries could change their economies. Because of this, he started working with the African heads of state to support their economic future with "discipline, knowledge, data, compliance, and good governance."

At that time, he was 32 and simultaneously climbing the corporate ladder to become CEO of DHL Freight. Tasked with managing mergers and acquisitions at Deutsche Post and DHL, he recalls how he was an unpopular choice with many employees. "There are lots of highly educated people in Germany with PhDs, and many Australians and Americans were already working at the company. They didn't like this young, stupid African sitting on the board, asking stupid questions." Another opportunity for him to impress.

Making a Better Place for All

Today, he is the CEO of DHL Global Forwarding for the Middle East and Africa, a position that has given him valuable exposure to a network of "old Dutch CEOs who played golf and knew a little bit about Africa." He meticulously studied how they thought and communicated, enabling an "underprivileged, small village guy" to gain insight into the inner workings and psyches of corporate tycoons. Again, for Amadou, everything is an opportunity.

Most strikingly, he's stayed true to himself and used his position to facilitate the early aims of that 16-year-old Senegalese activist. Believing that "you can use the

network and power of big corporations to influence people and create social impact." Amadou set up a global volunteering scheme through DHL that now has 130,000 people working on the ground to help local communities prosper and thrive.

Entrepreneurial Spirit

Even as a cow herder's son, it was evident Amadou was born with an entrepreneurial spirit; from selling shoes in a small shop to painting houses for immigrants living in poor conditions, he used every experience as a stepping stone. And, like most self-starters, he sees failure as part of success, "I never look at it as something you need to avoid, I look at it as an opportunity to improve".

Amadou's choice to utilise his entrepreneurial nature for the greater good rather than personal gain has had immeasurable effects on real people's livelihoods. Having spent the last 16 years integrating business in Asia, his motivation to carry on has always been the prosperity of the country and its people, rather than his own personal success. He explains that "for me, it is the best compensation, more than money or titles."

He suggests that "a lot of CEOs in companies talk about [social impact] but don't actually do it." Believing that physical activity is "the key to creating a society that aims to promote social impact." Alongside working with a number of NGO partners, he also has his own foundation in memory of his mother, who died when he was very young, and his grandmother, whom he describes as his main inspiration. Data from UNICEF indicates that children represent 48% of the total population in Senegal, so Amadou's foundation focuses on education for girls in southern Senegal, giving the next generation the opportunity and tools to thrive and make the world a better place.

Chilling

Amadou is clearly not your average corporate grey suit. An approachable, humorous, and yet deeply hardworking individual, he fully embodies the 'work hard, play hard' mantra. Admitting that he'll never stop working, he also confesses to being a party animal, with music, food, good company, and dancing being central to his well-being. "It liberates my brain, gives me good vibes, and inspires me. It's re-energising." Beyond his hectic slate of business and philanthropic responsibilities, he also likes to make music and is currently the producer for four different bands. And, in an attempt to fuse business, philanthropy, and music, he started a non-for-profit space in Senegal for people to gather, listen to music, eat, and chat. It seems that community is at the core of everything Amadou sets his sights on. What was once a focus on his neighbourhood in Kolda has spread to cover the whole world as a global community.

Nevertheless, Amadou has never forgotten his home, and wherever he has been in the world, he has taken Senegal with him. No matter which country he's working in, when he's finished for the day and walks through the door to his house, he is transported back to Senegal through the language, food, music, and art of his people. "Mobility is not about changing your culture, it's about feeling at home anywhere. You can be super mobile because you are always home." No matter how busy he is, he returns home at least once a year to be with his nine siblings and extended family, who all gather in his grandmother's old house.

Despite his life as a high-powered CEO, Amadou feels most content when he's lying under the shade of a tree on his family's farm, surrounded by cows. A highly intelligent, humble, and compassionate man who wants to be known as "a small village guy", who lives by a very simple mantra of "make money, respect people and have fun."

ANOUSHEH ANSARI

Astronaut, Tech Entrepreneur, Engineer | CEO - XPRIZE

The Dreamer

During the COVID-19 pandemic, we organized our first virtual conference for Facebook's Middle East and North Africa strategy. This conference brought together regional and global Facebook employees, leaders, and a wide range of exceptional speakers.

It was an honour for me to interview Anousheh at the event and hear her incredible story for the first time. I was amazed to learn about her journey from Iran to the United States and how she fulfilled her dream of travelling to space.

Furthermore, I was particularly interested to learn that she collaborates with Peter Diamandis, an international pioneer and innovator, as someone of Greek origin.

Anousheh is a truly inspirational person, and what impressed me the most was her ability to communicate complex topics using simple language.

> "My curiosity keeps me going. I always want to learn and do more, so I'm never satisfied with what I've done."

Growing up in Iran, Anousheh Ansari would spend the long, hot summer nights sleeping outside on her grandparents' balcony. An innately curious child, the stars sparkling against a velvety black night sky set Anousheh's imagination racing. As her young mind imagined faraway lands and civilizations, she wondered how she could one day reach them. In fact, it was the dream of space travel that sparked her interest in the more practical applications of maths and science. This eventually led to Anousheh obtaining a Bachelor's Degree in Electronics and Computer Engineering, a Master's Degree in Electrical Engineering, and 3 honorary doctorates.

Beyond academic excellence, Anousheh accomplished her childhood dream of becoming not only the first female private space explorer but the first Muslim woman in space, the fourth private space explorer, and the first astronaut of Iranian descent. As a 'spaceflight participant' she conducted a number of experiments and became the first person to publish a blog from space. Perhaps none of this would have happened if it hadn't been for those magical nights spent on her grandparents' balcony.

ANOUSHEH ANSARI
АНЮШЕ АНЗАРИ
SPACE
adventures

XPRIZE

In 2004, Anousheh helped launch the XPRIZE Foundation by sponsoring its first prize competition. Inspired by the organization's mission to empower humanity to achieve breakthroughs that accelerate an abundant future for all, Anousheh and her family sponsored the $10 million Ansari XPRIZE, designed to lower the risk and cost of space travel. The prize motivated 26 teams from 7 nations to invest $100m in new technologies in the hopes of benefiting the planet, and effectively launched a brand-new private space industry. After experiencing first-hand how XPRIZE could be a disruptor for good, Anousheh stayed involved with the organization, and after serving almost 20 years as a board member, she became its CEO around four years ago. The organization brings together exceptional teams of people across the globe, to compete to solve some of the most pressing issues facing humanity. Just a few examples of the XPRIZE's competitions including; developing new carbon removal technologies, finding sustainable ways to feed our growing population, turning carbon dioxide into usable products, mapping and healing the oceans, alleviating the global water crisis, and preserving the rainforests. For Anousheh, this has also given her a platform to make significant changes to the future of commercial spaceflight.

Stargazing

Her fascination with the universe has not diminished, and as she looks at pictures from the Hubble and James Webb telescopes, her fascination is palpable as she asserts "there are people like me who really grasp the magnitude of those images." It's this immensity that's difficult to convey to ordinary people and is only truly understood by the relatively few experts in the field of astrophysics. For Anousheh, looking at the universe gives her a different perspective on life, she has a greater understanding of just how small we are in comparison, which, in a way, allows her to deal with opportunities and failures with more optimism.

"Anything that I am talking about is possible."

> "Everyone is in their own little box and their own little world, and we create even more boxes and put ourselves in categories to separate from each other."

Anousheh has recorded her experiences of a life less ordinary in her memoir, 'My Dream of Stars'. It details her family's flight from Iran during the 1979 revolution and her building a technology company with a $750m net worth from scratch. The autobiography also documents her focus on social entrepreneurship and the empowerment of women. Her efforts to support and inspire other women have been realised through the Billion Dollar Fund for Women. Having been co-founded by Anousheh in 2018, it has already surpassed its $1 billion investment goal within nine months.

From Space, the World is Unified

This recent success and financial backing have encouraged a certain optimism when approaching big global problems. For Anousheh, the biggest issue in the world today is a feeling of disconnection. "Everyone is in their own little box and their own little world, and we create even more boxes and put ourselves in categories to separate from each other." She goes on to explain that people need to get rid of the imaginary boxes that separate them from each other because, from space, the world is unified, without borders and without labels defining gender, ethnicity, age, or religion. She wants people to realise this and work together to solve some of the world's biggest problems, focusing their energy on creating positive solutions. Anousheh believes that ultimately, we are all connected as humans inhabiting the same planet, and because of this, we need to find the things we have in common rather than the things that could divide us.

Earth and Beyond

XPRIZE is an endeavour that aligns very much with Anousheh's belief in collaboration and finding solutions to world's problems. As CEO of the foundation, she is focused on targeting climate change from various angles,

to make a collective impact. Their current active prizes include XPRIZE Wildfire, which will develop autonomous and space-based technologies to detect, manage, and put an end to destructive wildfires that increasingly wreak havoc on ecosystems, economies, and communities globally. To address the impacts of carbon emissions in our atmosphere and elsewhere, XPRIZE Carbon Removal encourages teams to find new ways to remove carbon dioxide, earth, and water to combat climate change and curb global warming. To protect and preserve rapidly diminishing rainforest ecosystems, XPRIZE Rainforest is spurring the development of technologies that can measure and evaluate biodiversity and support conservation efforts worldwide. And as the human population increases, so does the demand for meat products, which have harmful implications for the environment; XPRIZE Feed the Next Billion is designed to develop accessible and sustainable meat alternatives that outperform unsustainable chicken and fish products. It may sound like something out of science fiction, but by enabling teams across the world to approach problem-solving creatively through XPRIZE, otherwise improbably solutions become very real.

She is keen to point out that, instead of fighting each other, we need to start working together and putting our energy into building a wonderful society, as our species could become extinct if we continue to disrupt the delicate balance that keeps our planet alive. Anousheh reflects on the exponential growth in technology that she's been able to witness in her lifetime. Now, with the intersection of different technologies coming together, it's accelerating that rate of change and innovation to the point where she is certain that "anything that I am talking about is possible."

She discusses gene therapies and DNA sequencing with the casual ease of small talk. "Eventually, we will have to change our genes to be more resilient to radiation and the harsh environment of space, maybe the air." She adds that companies are already adding computer power to our brains, so we can connect our brains together and learn faster. It's all rather staggering and perhaps too much to take in, but for Anousheh, it's just a natural progression. Her only caveat is how the human race will respond to these immense technological advances, which could either enhance humanity or destroy it.

In the long term

Anousheh claims that the Middle East is particularly well suited to participate in ventures like XPRIZE because it has a younger generation that's hungry to build a more positive future. The area also has plenty of financial resources to be deployed, and they can afford to view things in the long term. Her organisation works with foundations, governments, individuals, and corporations - anyone who has an interest in the projects is welcome. Support can be varied, from financial help in launching competitions to becoming partners and providing services to the teams. Other forms of support can include manufacturing, legal advice, financial advice, and investment. Currently, 99% of investments are made with short-term targets and quick financial returns. However, Anousheh is keen to collaborate with those who want to leave a legacy.

Help or Hindrance

She has misgivings about the technologies that are rapidly evolving and being unleashed on the world, and worries that not enough time has been spent understanding their potential impact, whether positive or negative. She has other concerns too, mainly that most of the important technologies in the world are being created and controlled by just a handful of profit-driven companies whose aims and methods are going largely unchecked.

Alongside her many philanthropic endeavours, Anousheh spends much of her time and energy empowering young people. She truly believes that the youth are more capable, knowledgeable, willing, and caring about building a better future. Because of the internet, they're more informed and engaged, and as such, they can be powerful agents of change. This profound ability to connect through the digital world allows for accelerated levels of learning and sharing among the younger generations. There are more opportunities to collaborate and empathise. For Anousheh, with the right support and encouragement, we can build a stronger community for young people with the ability to grow and transform the world for the better.

APARNA ACHAREKAR

Co-Founder - coto

The Community Builder

Aparna came into my professional sphere when I joined coto as an advisor to the board for the MENA region. It was through a mutual acquaintance that I was introduced to Aparna and her Founder, Tarun, and we readily decided to collaborate for their expansion into the Middle East market. Given that Aparna was based in Mumbai, most of our interactions were done through virtual means such as Zoom calls. However, we eventually met in person during the official launch of coto in Dubai a few months later. Our interaction was very enjoyable, and it felt like a natural connection when working together.

"I came from a well-educated, forward-thinking family, so there was never a gender division in terms of the opportunities I wanted to pursue."

Aparna co-founded coto (Eve World) in response to the amount of gender bias she witnessed in the sphere of business. It's a decentralised, safe, virtual community made for women, by women. The social community platform built on web3 principles exclusively targets women to encourage mentorship, free expression, and networking. "It's all about helping women develop their identity and sense of independence and inclusion." Understanding first-hand the unique struggles of being a modern woman, like balancing family life with an ambitious career, coto aims to support female entrepreneurs, facilitate upskilling, and provide a wide range of specialist information.

Medicine to Media

From an early age, Aparna understood that her first competitor was herself. Something she still teaches her fifteen-year-old son is the analogy of an athlete constantly working to beat their personal best. So, for Aparna, continuous improvement is a necessary part of life. With this in mind, she had the will and confidence to break free from expected gender roles in India during the early 90s and graduated with a Degree in Microbiology and Biotechnology, with aspirations of becoming a doctor. Nevertheless, she quickly realised that surrounding herself with blood and pain on a daily basis wasn't for her. So, she went back to school and graduated with a postgraduate degree in Mass Communication and an MBA in Business, smashing her 'personal best.'

Sometimes, timing is everything, and the media industry was beginning to boom in India, resulting in plenty of opportunities opening up for Aparna. Her first role was as a journalist for The Times of India, where she was able to capitalise on her excellent communication skills. Being provided the opportunity to cover stories about her community, speak to a wide range of diverse people, and learn how they lived began to change her perspective on life. She began to realise that "the glamour and materialism that everyone seeks [are] just superficial. It's the real people who truly matter." As a journalist, she really cared and would spend hours trying to understand the complexity of just one person's story, often meaning that these stories would stay with her long afterwards.

She remembers once writing a piece about breast cancer. After it had been published, she received a call from a man who had read the article, noticed his wife had similar symptoms, and pushed her to go to the doctor – a sequence of events that ultimately saved her life. Perhaps then, she had not strayed too far from her original 'reason why' because "it's not necessarily the big things that are changing the planet, it's also the smaller impacts made on individuals." For Aparna, we often neglect the little things because we're constantly striving for bigger purposes and goals. Even if at the time she felt her article was inconsequential, her ability to communicate with people changed the course of at least two people's lives forever.

"It's not necessarily the big things that
are changing the planet, it's also the
smaller impacts made on individuals."

Eve World

When discussing gender equality, Aparna suggests that the goal shouldn't be equality, "I don't want to be equal to anybody." Instead, it should be focused on giving women the freedom to choose as individuals. "It shouldn't matter if a woman's happiness lies in being a great home-maker or pursuing a career, what matters is that she be allowed to achieve it." So, it's a matter of freedom, self-expression and, ultimately, a sense of fulfilment, that she aims to facilitate, and she believes society has a role to play in someone's ability to express themselves authentically.

Aparna's own sense of individual fulfilment was an important factor in her decision to become an entrepreneur, this choice was guided by a need to help women achieve the same feeling in their own lives. This is why she co-founded Eve World/ coto, a social community platform built specifically to empower and help women express themselves freely and authentically. With facial recognition and multifactor authentication to ensure a safe online environment for women to communicate with each other, Eve World/ coto is all about "building an ecosystem that empowers and engages women". In creating a new digital world where they can seek mentorship and connection both freely and safely, Aparna is hoping to break down all barriers that might prevent women from pursuing their dreams.

Faith in God and Faith in Oneself

It is evident that Aparna is deeply appreciative of her parents' support, and understanding of her privileged upbringing. However, ultimately, she believes that she is following the path God set out for her. Although there have been times when she has felt overwhelming fear on this journey, her faith allows her to remain grounded and determined with the mantra, "if fear is on one side of her heart, there is reassurance on the other." When she made the difficult choice to quit medicine after studying for so long, knowing deep down that she couldn't deal with pain on a daily basis, her positive attitude and "faith in divine guidance" gave her the courage to throw herself into a new challenge with the belief that "the sense of insecurity or feeling that you're not good enough soon dissipates with positive affirmation."

This trust in one's path and oneself is something she tries to instil in her son. "My focus as a parent is to raise a child who is independent and stands up for his decisions." Nevertheless, she acknowledges the need for community, being quick to praise her husband for his loyal support, particularly as a successful woman juggling a career and family life.

"The sense of insecurity or feeling
that you're not good enough soon
dissipates with positive affirmation."

Better to Give than Receive

Aparna's approach is always more focused on the human transaction than the outcome. When she asks herself what would make her happy, the answer usually comes down to what would make others happy. She maintains that "giving is the best form of receiving; it's the transfer of kindness." And it's this feeling of collective responsibility that has really driven her career choices, pushing her to focus less on individual pursuits and more on uplifting her community so that we all grow together.

"Giving is the best form
of receiving; it's the
transfer of kindness."

FARES AKKAD

Regional Director for Meta, MEA

The 'Entrepreneur at heart'

Although I had worked alongside Fares for some time, we weren't particularly close. Our interactions were limited to occasional conversations during various projects. Fares was someone I could easily chat with and then not see for some time.

However, I had the opportunity to get to know him better when he assumed the role of Managing Director for Middle East and Africa at Meta (formerly Facebook). At that time, I was responsible for the People and Culture of the MENA team, in addition to my business role. We spent many hours with Fares redesigning our People and Culture strategy, particularly as we had returned from the Covid-19 pandemic and were attempting to encourage people to return to the office. Fares is a person who means business and is fully committed to what he does. He has a clear short and long-term action plan and a soft spot for people.

"If you don't challenge yourself, you don't grow."

Born in Brazil to Syrian parents with a father in the diplomatic service, Fares has had a unique start in life with lots of travel and exposure to different cultures, including Latin America, Syria, London, Spain, the US, and now Dubai. The diversity of lifestyle and culture at such a young age has left a deep impression on Fares, who is able to see the commonalities across a wide range of different cultures, serving him well in friendships and in business.

The first time I met Fares, I was impressed by how calm he looked. Being in a meeting room with him, you feel your pulse slow down, focus on the key points that need attention, and make actionable decisions. I think his "entrepreneurial background" helps him be the cool guy.

For Fares, a week or two of sightseeing is just not enough to appreciate a culture. He believes that in order for us to understand our global "commonalities" we need to truly immerse ourselves in different communities. As a child, he confronted the challenges of moving to a new country many times over; making new friends, learning new languages, and getting used to new lifestyles. These initial struggles ultimately developed Fares' ability to identify what unites us all, allowing him to build bridges of communication with ease.

New Challenges

Having lived in a range of different countries throughout his childhood, Fares has mastered the skill of quickly putting down roots in a new place while also being prepared to leave again. His constant pursuit of new experiences and exploring the unfamiliar also determines his career choices, and he admits to feeling an innate need for a jolt or a new challenge at least every 4 or 5 years. And, as the General Manager for META (Middle East and Africa), his latest and perhaps greatest challenge has already begun.

As a leader in the metaverse, communication is at the very core of everything Fares does, and it's no surprise that he is "attracted to transformative things at the edge or really relevant to people's lives." After working for a space start-up, he shifted into consulting and experienced "a lot of interest in the intersection between media and tech." It appears his formal education also prepared him well for this career. With degrees in BioTech and Information Systems, he joined a media group focused primarily on the technology of space, before moving to META to be at the "cutting edge of human interest and development."

It may seem serendipitous that Fares found META, or indeed, that META found him, because both have a focus on digital communication. Noticing early on that everything was "going digital and social", he immediately recognized the relevance of META and was excited by the "ambiguity and uncertainty" that often come from relevancy.

> "Technology has always been an extension of how society wants to communicate."

"The metaverse will eventually reflect how we interact in society. "

Human Connection

Fares considers himself an "extrovert", but there are times when he is more "reserved" and needs that "anchor" called home, a place he goes back to each night. Although "home is very important" to Fares, he nonetheless, truly values human connection and interaction. Rather than "polite cocktail conversation", he gets a lot of fulfillment from deep and meaningful exchanges, striving to "touch people on a personal level."

When discussing the metaverse, he's excited by the prospect of it being able to overcome "our subconscious bias." With an upbeat and positive attitude toward the consequences, he suggests that "technology has always been an extension of how society wants to communicate." For Fares, the metaverse offers us a unique chance to present ourselves in the way we wish to be perceived. He hopes this will promote diversity and inclusion while making interactions between people more based on merit than appearance or status.

He projects that the metaverse will eventually "reflect how we interact in society." Acknowledging the risks this could entail, he focuses instead on the positives, like potentially creating "a lot of opportunity for people to better express themselves and overcome some preconceived notions."

The field of media technology is notoriously precarious and fluid, and in order to thrive despite constant and rapid changes, you need to have trust in your decisions. Fares claims this comes with experience. "It's this kind of dynamic between you and your conscience, when you have faith in yourself, you become more courageous to take bigger risks." He compares life to a game, and accolades like money, titles, and recognition are all part of the scoreboard. He knows the game is sometimes based on sheer luck, but he is also aware that "taking lemons and making lemonade is a skill."

Consistency is underrated

One of the consequences of moving around frequently, apart from becoming comfortable with "ambiguity and uncertainty", is that you tend to appreciate consistency a little more. For Fares, that's his family and his home. Now, as a father of two young children, he is keen to emulate his own childhood setting, which was "a safe place, a warm place, and a place where my parents [were] always available."

Now he's found that perfect home in Dubai, where he's lived for a decade. As a family man with young children, he appreciates the feeling of "safety and peace of mind when they're out and about" and welcomes the "secure and service-oriented" aspects of the city. As a business leader, he recognises the "massive transformation" in Qatar, Saudi Arabia, the UAE, and Egypt in recent years and aspires to leverage the opportunity to have an impact on the region and the community in the future.

Fares believes that providing a secure home is important, but building his children's confidence is essential "for their self esteem, decision-making skills, willingness to take risks, and resilience in failure... it stems from an array of things, including feeling love, being encouraged, and being prepared."

It's a work in progress, but ultimately, he wants his children to focus on what they can change. "Life throws all sorts of curveballs at you, and there is a very narrow space in which you can operate." He identifies with more logical approaches to problem solving and suggests that issues should be dealt with systematically, through prioritization and focus because "there's something rewarding about it. It's Stoic philosophy, but I firmly believe in it."

> "For us to understand our global 'commonalities', we need to truly immerse ourselves in different communities."

Leveraging Opportunities

As a shrewd business leader, he believes that success is fundamentally all about confidence, accepting that "most things you try have higher chances of failing than succeeding." He suggests it's not about being optimistic or pessimistic, "it's more about making your best bets". Fares is assured in his ability to go from beginner to expert in under 18 months, regardless of the industry. His confidence has definitely grown throughout his career, mainly because he has purposely placed himself in challenging situations, grown from the experience, and learned to trust himself a little more. With that also comes a heightened awareness of "what works for you". For Fares, having mentors is a great fit for his personal working style, as he appreciated being able to think out loud to a sounding board.

While he feels he could eventually become indifferent to failure, his family keeps him focused, "when I think about it, it's actually more the fear of failing your loved ones". He's constantly trying to maintain balance and security within an industry that requires flexibility amidst instability. His career advice is to "fast forward two years and look back", not to dwell on any regrets, but to learn from your mistakes and to gain a better understanding of yourself and how things work, so you can then "look forward and project how things will play out." He is an entrepreneur at heart.

"Taking lemons and making
lemonade is a skill."

JOE FOSTER

Founder of Reebok

The Shoemaker

Joe's visit to Dubai a few years ago for his book launch was when I first discovered his extraordinary life story. He embodies a vibrant force, full of life and energy, distinguished not only by his past achievements but even more so by his future aspirations. His response to what he plans next – "I want to do more" – reflects the youthful vigor and clear vision that define him. Joe's strength is further amplified by the unwavering support of his loving wife Julie, his constant companion and source of inner power.

Joe Foster's life is a remarkable one, spanning decades and continents, with drama, suspense, tragedy, and humour. His autobiography, 'Shoemaker' is an epic account of his personal and entreprencurial highs and lows, with experiences that have now led him to becoming a globally renowned industry celebrity. The charming, humble, and very English gentleman is the creator of Reebok, which he started in a modest factory in Bolton. His quiet demeanour and modest presence belie the powerful, shrewd, and dynamic executive and, in a real David and Goliath story, Mr Foster has been elevated to legendary status. Having gone against the giant beasts of Adidas and Nike, Joe didn't just create an iconic brand, he left a living legacy.

<blockquote>
"If you're the most intelligent person in the room, you're in the wrong room."
</blockquote>

The making of a gentleman

Joe's great-grandfather repaired shoes for cricketers and taught the craft of cobbling to Joe's grandfather, who later went on to found his company, J W Foster, in 1895, forty years before Joe was born. Joe's grandfather, who made running shoes, in fact, developed one of the first track spikes. The company was well respected for performance and quality and reached its heyday in the 1920s, producing some of the most highly regarded performance running shoes. The 100m Olympic Champion, Harold Abrahams (of 'Chariots of Fire' fame), wore the revolutionary spiked shoes in Paris in 1924. Running shoes were in his DNA, and so it was inevitable that Joe and his brother would one day come to work in the business. But it was not inevitable, or perhaps even conceivable, that J W Foster would become Reebok.

When World War II started, Joe was 4 years old, and he still reminisces on the times he would "head down into the air raid shelter" with his friends, like it was all part of an exciting game. At 17, he did what was expected of sons at the time, and joined the family business. However, he explains, "I was really more interested in socialising with girls and enjoying my new-found freedom." Nevertheless, the dutiful son spent one year learning the business, until he was called up to do national service. He spent two years in the RAF as a radar operator and learned that he "could ask questions and seek ways of making things different." He also delighted in the fact that he could spend much of his time playing badminton.

When his brother Jeff did his national service in Germany, he was able to observe the developments that Adidas and Puma were making in the sports footwear market. And on returning to the failing family business, with two co-founding brothers in the middle of a feud, Joe and Jeff had only one course of action, "Jeff and I decided to leave the family business and set up on our own together."

"Money should never be the
driving force...business is always
recognising what other people need."

> "The secret to success in business is to keep looking for the drive and the next challenge."

Proverbs and Prophecy

Joe now pays it forward through mentoring and, with a mix of knowledge, curiosity, experience and an acceptance of how fast things move, he's the perfect mentor. He embraces innovation and technology, still looking for the revolutionary material that will provide the perfect cushion for your feet. Perhaps surprisingly, his social media presence is as varied as any influencer's.

"The question in my mind was always, how do you get a company to grow? If it doesn't grow, it stagnates or plateaus. And once you plateau, the most likely thing is that you go down because you lose the drive." For Joe, the secret to success in business is to "keep looking for the drive and the next challenge." In his eighties, he has written an autobiography and still embraces technology and global travel with the energy of a man half his age.

Joe is testament to his dictum that "money should never be the driving force." Performance was his driving force, and perhaps to be the best, but now that he has achieved both, what else is there for this clever and charismatic man? "For me, business is always recognising what other people need." What Joe has recognised is the need to feel comfortable in what you wear, to the extent that even brides may favour wearing trainers over heels. He therefore advises the new owners of Reebok, ABG, to "be looking at the future", suggesting that all sportswear companies are basically now in fashion and that the main competitors, "Nike and Adidas, drive their sports companies through performance, music, and the street."

Joe has an abundance of wisdom, that he's more than happy to pass down to any entrepreneurs. He leads the way for a more philanthropic style of entrepreneurship, emphasising that "the driving force should be what we can make and leave in this world, more than money." It's really about finding purpose, which is where the business world is heading. He also has progressive and practical advice for business leaders. "When employing people, listen to what they can bring and let them participate." Astute advice and somewhat visionary considering that collaboration is the buzzword in the workplace. It's clear that Joe is a people person, "your future depends on other people and on making those relationships."

Now 88 years old, there is definitely a sense that the sequel is already in production. The epic chronicles of Joe Foster continue with travels around the world to many and varied locations, plus another book series in the works, and the same passion he had when starting out all those decades ago.

> "Your future depends on other people
> and on making those relationships."

KIRTHIGA REDDY

Co-founder & CEO - Virtualness

The Doer

There is nothing Kirthiga cannot do. When we were working together at Facebook, she was based out of San Francisco and I was based in Dubai. She was ready to take super late or super early calls, to accommodate everyone on the team, and make stuff happen. She is one of these people that you can build trust and respect in no time, and you know you can reach out at any given moment. One of my favourite moments was when we were both at one of the global sales conferences with Facebook in San Francisco in 2016. At that time, Kirthiga was the global lead for one of our top 10 clients, and I was the regional head for financial services and automotive. We were all super exhausted from the time difference, the all day-long conference, the constant running from meeting to meeting, and we had to present our next year's strategy for the client we were working together. This meeting was one of the best meetings I ever had. It was the definition of team spirit and leadership.

"Today I am an entrepreneur, investor, board member, and mum."

A bold visionary, perpetual learner, successful business builder, and mother of two, Kirthiga Reddy is a champion of women who see their destiny across the worlds of enterprise, education, and philanthropic endeavours.

As a young girl growing up in a middle-class Indian family, Kirthiga was a strong academic student who developed a passion for engineering. "I found it magical to go from a problem statement, analyse it, apply technology, and solve a problem." It was this passion and talent that took her on an incredible journey of once-in-a lifetime opportunities.

Her odyssey began after she completed a Master's in Computer Engineering in the US. She spent six years at Silicon Graphics Inc., a leader in technological innovation involved in the making of the film Jurassic Park, the Human Genome Project, and landing on Mars.

EVEREST BASE CAMP
5380 masl
feui 91

From Facebook to WeWork

She realised that she really enjoyed the business side of engineering and then secured an MBA from Stanford University, a milestone that she considers to be one of the most transformative decisions of her life. It allowed her to diversify her skills and learn more about product management, which she used to secure a new role at a start-up acquired by Motorola. By that time, she was married with two young daughters and had moved back to India, where she was introduced to Sheryl Sandberg, the COO of Facebook. A 'builder' at heart, Kirthiga pitched the idea of constructing Facebook's operations in India.

Almost a year later, Facebook decided to open its first office in India, and following an intense interview process, Kirthiga was appointed as the first employee in the role of Managing Director. Her risk-taking attitude, focus on culture and enterprise expertise resulted in establishing one of Facebook's four global operations offices that together serve over 3.5B users. She also built Facebook's Asia Pacific Small Medium Business Revenue to several $100Ms in annual revenue on a path to several billion. Similarly, she built Facebook's India revenue to several $100Ms in annual revenue and secured investments to grow it to a revenue of over a billion dollars. "Just being part of a country that was going digital and mobile and seeing the impact that it had on people, businesses, and society was truly transformational for me."

However, she "missed the start-up ecosystem, which really led her to that very hard decision to leave Facebook." After almost 8 years at Facebook, she changed direction and started her own seed fund. As SoftBank Vision Fund's first female investment partner, she was able to help young businesses grow. She spent 3 successful years at SoftBank Investment Advisers, deploying over a billion dollars, and joining the board of WeWork as part of their business turnaround. "I feel very grateful to have had the opportunity to work with incredible entrepreneurs across the globe who are transforming the way we live and work."

"It truly takes a 'village' when it comes to having ambitious goals in life."

It can't be done alone

"My family has always been a source of support, and it truly takes a 'village' when it comes to having ambitious goals in life." Kirthiga's strength is strongly rooted in her relationship with her family. Dev Reddy has been a stalwart husband throughout her career transitions. When she was agonizing about whether she should pursue an MBA education or not, he encouraged her to go for it, reminding her that regretting what she has done is better than regretting what she has not done. Her mother, who did not have the opportunity to finish high school, has been an important part of Kirthga's journey and has remained a pinnacle of support. Travelling alone on a plane from India to help Kirthiga when she was pregnant with her first child was a courageous and bold deed and reflects the can-do attitude that Kirthiga grew up witnessing. As a working mother and wife, she has also refrained from keeping her professional life separate from her home life, "I am a full-time professional, a full-time mother, a full-time wife, a full-time daughter, and a full-time friend, and I'm playing these roles in every single moment." It is this approach that has enabled her to have such a successful work-life balance.

ATEK.U
LISTED
NYSE
ΑΤΗΣΝΑ

The Challenges of Bias

In the early years of her career, the concepts of a glass ceiling and gender discrimination were unfamiliar territory. However, as she moved into more senior positions, she became more conscious of systematic bias, stereotyping, and barriers because she began to experience them on a personal level as a woman in business. "Even at senior levels, some people will tell you they believe you got the role because you were a woman, not because of the impact you have made." Her own personal encounters have supported evidence to suggest that men get promoted based on potential, whereas women get promoted based on performance. She notes that she's had to work much harder when championing a female leader for promotion compared to their male counterparts. "I've seen examples where the woman has had to wait almost another year to be promoted."

Thinking Back and Doing It Differently

"If I've done something wrong, I use it as a learning moment to see how I can improve." The shifting paradigm around diversity and the 'me too' movement has had an indubitable impact on both society and business. Kirthiga has noted a change in her own attitude, she now feels more empowered to stand up for herself with the knowledge that everyone is more enlightened to the issues at hand, explaining that "one side is women finding their courage to speak out, and the other side is those in power being more receptive."

She highlights a first-hand example where an external Senior Executive consistently addressed a male co-worker while ignoring her, despite the fact that they were both introduced as key decision makers. Having the courage to call attention to this issue with a polite but focused email to the Senior Executive was a small but important step that sparked a change in attitude. But Kirthiga also suggests that everyone has a personal responsibility to increase their awareness of bias, stereotyping, and barriers. She recommends educating yourself by reading, listening to podcasts and "of course, Golden Nuggets." She stipulates that driving diversity, equity, and inclusion initiatives has been as important as talking about deploying a billion dollars or managing a portfolio worth over $5 billion.

In 2022, Kirthiga became part of the first all-female, all immigrant team ringing the New York Stock Exchange's opening IPO bell, as part of leading Athena Technology II Special Purpose Acquisition Company (SPAC). Made all the more special by having her two teenage daughters on the podium with her while her mother dialled in from India, it was an appropriately female affair for a woman so focused on championing other women. "It is just remarkable how much difference one generation can make. And also a reminder of the change we need to drive for the next generation."

At Softbank Vision Fund, diversity, equity, and inclusion initiatives mean creating affinity groups to ensure underrepresented groups have strong voices. Additionally, championing platforms like Connect-and-Lead generated networking opportunities by bringing women from across the portfolio together. Finally, sponsoring Emerge has been a great accelerator programme for companies with diverse founders.

"Diversity is very visible, but inclusion is the next frontier of the challenge leaders need to think about." As chair of the Stanford Business School Management Board, Kirthiga saw first-hand the emerging challenges with inclusion practices: What are the processes? What if people from different nationalities don't agree? What if there are fundamental differences based on religion? What happens if someone is from a country where their religion doesn't allow them to be lesbian or gay, but that's their individual identity? Diversity is about being invited to the dance floor. Equity is about provisions, so everyone can dance. Inclusion is - are you dancing? And then belonging - can you dance however you want to without having to fit into norms?"

The definition of being underrepresented

Kirthiga suggests that diversity and inclusion come in different forms. While working at Facebook India, she noticed that the larger operations groups had strong connections and a shared sense of identity just from working together. However, she identified that more effort was needed to ensure that those individuals working alone could also experience that same sense of connection, "it's in the small and the big, and it's about recognizing diversity and inclusion in their various forms".

NYSE CLOSING BELL
AUGUST 26, 2022
LADDRR
Stepping Up Careers Of Ten Million Moms
LADDRR
Stepping Up Careers Of Ten Million Moms
NEW YORK STOCK EXCHANGE
4:01:39
CNBC
NYSE
CNBC
NYSE

She noticed a pattern where people were only being hired from other major social media platforms and search engines. With diversity and inclusion in mind, she ensured that a wider group was hired from radio, television, and print to expand the skill sets. "I cannot emphasise enough the role of leaders in being able to strongly champion the need for diversity and inclusion." She believes there is power in a community where people can share their stories with each other, "it speaks to the core of what you are doing here with One Golden Nugget and this book."

The key to business success

"For me, you cannot be successful in business if you're not successful with people", and it's this community-focused approach that she learned from her time at Facebook. Since then, her philosophy has been focused on "hiring the right people and building the right culture", a practice she believes will inevitably lead to business results. This is how she's approached her own businesses throughout her career, and, in a post-pandemic climate, this currency of care has become more important than ever.

The New Generation and Global Challenges

Witnessing the value systems of next-generation business builders, Kirthiga notes a shift from 'the bigger, the better' to a more principled, purpose-driven approach. Recent studies suggest that the "why" behind business is a core driving factor for the next generation of entrepreneurs. She's been impressed with how the next generation is evolving in their philosophies and expectations, and she believes that it's crucial for companies to now grow alongside them.

Out of the many challenges that face society on a global scale, she names climate change as the most critical. The recent political debate around abortion rights in the US has also shone a major spotlight on the enduring issue of women's rights. "It's shocking that I'm sitting here in the United States, one of the richest countries by GDP, and we're having this discussion about women's rights. As a nation, we are rallying together to fight this, and it's been incredible to see the enormous support we've had from across the world." The younger generation's commitment to maintaining and fighting for their rights has calmed her anxieties. Kirthiga understands it was her generation that created many of the issues. This generation needs to course correct - with urgency! And she encourages the next generation to bring their passion, expertise and fresh ideas to challenge the status quo and drive change at scale.

Legacy

Kirthiga has decades of fighting left to help solve global issues, but fundamentally, she would like to be known for building businesses, "because when businesses succeed, livelihoods flourish." Her legacy also has a more personal note to it, where she wants every person who interacts with her to know how special they are to her and "feel that they learned something that is helpful and valuable to them."

On an even more personal note, she wants to be known for being a mother, wife, daughter, and friend. When one of her daughters once said that she knew that no matter how busy her mother was and how many demands work placed on her, she knew that she came first, it was a heart stopping accolade for Kirthiga, "I couldn't ask for more."

"When businesses succeed,
livelihoods flourish."

MELINA TAPRANTZI

Founder - Wise Greece
United Nations "SDGs and Her Award" winner

The Social Entrepreneur

Melina is a remarkable woman with global recognition of her social entrepreneurship and her social impact in Greece and on a global scale.

During my interview with Melina, she was only a few days away from giving birth to her first child. We chatted extensively about various topics such as Greece's economy, immigration and social entrepreneurship, and her remarkable endeavours to empower women and youth.

Melina's focused mission to bring about social change left me completely captivated.

"Every social enterprise that
respects itself wouldn't want
to be alive in five years."

Describing herself as a "socialist governor and entrepreneur at heart, with purpose and mission", Melina was a recipient of the World Bank and UN's award 'Sustainable Development Goals and Her' in 2020. She's a keynote speaker on social entrepreneurship, a TEDX speaker, and an ambassador of the 'Think Young Entrepreneurship School', so she certainly lives up to her aims.

From a more general perspective, one could say that her motivation to reach this point was formulated during her Philosophy degree, which was "vague, wide, and diverse, about everything and nothing at the same time." Yet, more specifically, it was really a series of completely unexpected events that really catapulted her into the world of social entrepreneurship.

Initially, Melina's career path seemed pretty conventional. Starting out in a couple of different advertising agencies, working in both creative and strategy, she went on to co-found her own agency in 2007, called 'Add Honey'. Things were going well until the debt crisis of 2010, but little did she know that a chance visit to a grocery store in the midst of economic upheaval would start a rollerball of activity to save the Greek economy and feed the hungry.

The Sinking Ship

In 2010, austerity measures left 22% of the population unemployed and a third living below the poverty line. Many people living in Greece felt they had no option but to leave a "dying economy" in search of a better future. However, Melina Trapantzi remained, determined to do something good amidst the chaos and suffering that had consumed the country.

While most of the world watched events unfold in front of their TVs, Melina was watching first-hand. People in a country known for food and tourism were going hungry. On research, she found that food insecurity was a massive problem across Europe, not just in Greece, with "500,000 people depending on soup kitchens for a meal" in the UK alone. Shocked at the numbers, she was still determined not to be a helpless bystander, knowing in her heart that "there must be a way of doing well and doing good at the same time."

Wise Greece

The concept of social enterprise, being both financially successful and doing good for society, was not something Melina was familiar with at the time. All she knew was that she "wanted to do something different, like create a new model that would be financially sustainable but would have a maximum social impact." And that new business model was formed with the founding of 'Wise Greece' in 2016, a social enterprise initiative that helps local farmers grow, sell, and feed "people in need." The aim is to promote Greek products, then use the profits to buy food to donate to soup kitchens, children, families, and the elderly. It's a perfect example of social entrepreneurship because it's both financially sustainable and impactful. In this case, it's not only the small farmers who benefit from exporting their products but also those in need of food.

Nevertheless, farmers were suspicious, and there was a general feeling of mistrust throughout the country at the time, so getting the project off the ground was difficult for Melina, who spent months trying to persuade farmers to come on board. However, once she won their trust, things started to move quickly in the right direction.

It's a simple idea that is now being adopted on a global scale, and it's not surprising such a valuable endeavour has won so many awards, including the 'Models of Excellence' award by the President of the Greek Republic, the 'StartUp Greece' award, and the 'Voluntary Action' award. To date, Wise Greece has shipped 2500 products to 8 countries in the EU and US markets and donated over 110 tons of food to orphanages, soup kitchens, and charitable institutions.

> "You start with the social problem, you identify the problem, then you start building a business plan around it, and you solve it."

Cottage Industry

Once the project was successfully up and running, Melina began to look at long-term goals. "We started realising that giving away food is not enough, you need to do something to educate the next generation and support the unemployed people around Greece. So, we started organising educational courses."

Melina noticed that there was an untapped cottage industry in Greece. Women in the villages would cook dishes every day in their homes and just give them away to friends and family. So she launched an educational programme to teach them about entrepreneurship and how to monetise their untapped potential. "They had never heard of the terms business plan, marketing plan, or financial plan, but after attending the seminars, they started understanding the benefits of using those tools." To date, the organisation has educated 1400 men and women aged between 18-30, not just empowering them in business but encouraging them to think of themselves as integral to Greece's food and tourism industries.

She hopes that her social enterprises will encourage people to stay in Greece and find success without compromising their homes and families. "We need to cultivate their understanding that you don't have to leave the country, or even your village, because you can create a job right where you are, you can stay there, get an income, give jobs to other people, and so forth."

10
wise
GREECE!
0 XPONIA WISE GREECE

Oregano and Solar Panels

It's not just the Greek economy that she has her sights on, global sustainability practices are also at the top of her list, and she currently works with a few companies in Europe and Africa on their environmental, social, and governance pillars. "Companies have started realising that it's about creating social value. It's about creating a lasting footprint, wherever we are."

Melina worked as a consultant for other companies focusing on the S&G of ESG (environmental, social and governance) programs because they were measurable results.

Melina currently works for ENEL, one of Italy's main power supplies, which happens to own a football club in Kozani, Greece. Before she was brought in, the company used to give away money to locals and the mayor as a charitable donation. Even though it had no actual social impact, it kept "everybody happy". So, the company approached Melina for her expertise in creating social impact by investing in the next generation. It was decided that they would support the unemployed women in Kozani, Syria, and allow them to plant herbs under photovoltaic panels. Melina suggests, "it proves the agricultural sector and the renewable energy sector can coexist, they don't have to co-exist."

Money and the Planet

Melina wants to shift the entrepreneurial focus away from wanting to create the next shiny new technology and towards social enterprise. Referring to the latest World Economic Forum, she believes this will help mitigate current job shortages due to technology and immigration issues.

She looks to GenZs and Millennials who want to "combine the efficiency and the power to take care of the environment and the world along with making money", and claims Greece to be a "paradise for any social entrepreneur" with all its "many social problems." Her model is simple, "you start with the social problem, you identify the problem, then you start building a business plan around it, and you solve it." It's clear that Melina has found a great sense of worth in her many enterprises, and now has the time to appreciate what she's been able to achieve in the face of such global adversities.

NADER BASTAKI

Strategy & Development at Dubai Future District Fund
Early-Stage Tech Investments & Advisory in Dubai and MENA

The Traveler

Nader embodies the essence of futuristic technologies, innovation, and sustainable development. His insatiable curiosity drives him to seek continuous growth and progress in order to find fulfillment. A natural conversationalist, Nader effortlessly engages in discussions spanning a wide range of topics, effortlessly delving deep into complex subjects while maintaining a broad perspective. His openness and willingness to explore diverse ideas, an area so close to my heart, make him a captivating and thought-provoking individual to converse with.

"One of the key enablers to making startups in the ecosystem happen is bringing amazing people together."

Having already accomplished so much at such a young age, it's clear that the best is yet to come for Nader Bastaki. As the acting Chief of Strategy for the Dubai Future Foundation, he's at the heart of shaping Dubai's future, a city he's called home for the past three years.

Nader has visited an impressive 127 countries to date, and with an educational background spanning across three different continents, he's certainly well-equipped to bridge cultural gaps. For him, "the idea of getting exposure to different people, different perspectives, different mindsets, and different lenses of looking at different things has an educational value to it."

This global experience is undoubtedly an advantage when it comes to widening perspectives and opening minds. However, Nader acknowledges the merits of being able to ground this experience in a formal education, "in academic circles, people think in very abstract ways about the world... I was taught to be curious."

It was this curiosity that pushed him to pursue a degree in Economics at the University of Waterloo, an experience he considers pivotal as "it was an entrepreneurial hub, the Silicon Valley of Canada." Nader describes being surrounded by a large number of start-ups as exciting and contagious. And, infected with an "innovative and entrepreneurial mindset", he started his own cosmetics distribution company, describing how his "timing couldn't have been better, the overall macroeconomic environment really helped its growth and my eventual exit from it."

Large Corps and Start-Ups

After obtaining his degree, Nader had a number of opportunities placed at his feet but chose to follow a corporate career with HSBC because of the "way that they tackle CSR, they didn't boast about it, they just did it." He was particularly impressed by the company's corporate social responsibility strategies, "It was amazing to be not just joining a massive organisation, but one that cared and gave back to the communities." The educational value of this experience had also not been lost on Nader, "in the process of working in this organisation, you're around great leaders and great mindsets." Working for such a huge corporation offered him a solid platform and a thorough understanding of "what works in the business world." Like many born-to-be businessmen, his entrepreneurial spirit returned, and he founded the health tech start-up 'Alchemize'. Another situation of 'right place, right time', Dubai was going through another growth cycle. "There was a lot of movement into the country, a lot of money, numerous new people, and new opportunities."

Bridging Cultural Gaps

In 2015, Nader was conscripted into the army, an initiative that evolved in the UAE to "bridge cultural gaps, bring unity, and also bring togetherness in the Emirati population." In typical style, he approached the experience with a positive mindset, "I got exposed to plenty of people doing countless amazing things... and it made me start challenging myself in different ways." Reflecting on the opportunity, he describes the profound effect it had on his outlook, "I'd never had the exposure to different parts of society, doing different things, with different ambitions in life." With a natural curiosity, Nader became interested in working for more grassroots organisations around the world, leading him to become involved with the Nepalese NGO 'Smile for Hope', an initiative that helped supply medical relief to rural areas following the Kathmandu earthquake.

As a tiny local NGO that was started by someone who had climbed to the base camp of Mount Everest, built relationships with the Sherpas over the years, and decided to give back to the community, Nader was truly inspired by the way such a small organisation was able to save and shape so many lives.

Nader's NGO

Eighteen months later, in August 2017, a conflict sent hundreds of thousands of Rohingya Muslims fleeing across the border into Bangladesh. So, inspired by 'Smile for Hope', Nader started his own foundation "to help people who are in the most desperate of times." He recounts, "I went to Cox's Bazar, to the refugee camp, just after about 300,000 people arrived. There was USAID, the Red Cross, the Red Crescent, and a number of these massive global entities. But one thing I noticed was that they were only focused on the infrastructure. They were giving them a roof over their heads, sanitary equipment, and utensils, but one thing was missing, the most basic of needs - food."

He explains how the area was "ripe for friction", as arable land around the border of Myanmar was scarce and a number of farmers had been pushed out to make space for the refugee camps. However, as a natural problem-solver, he viewed the source of friction as a possible solution.
"The idea was to source [food] locally, so you get the buy-in of the farmers", and also provide food for the refugees. "It's not a massive set-up, but it's something that I wanted to build up just for my own sake, the tiny little bits and pieces of impact that you can create along the way".

Moving Forward to Get Ahead

Looking at Nader's journey so far, he's a man who requires constant growth and forward movement to feel fulfilled. In his fast-paced

world, there's little room for 'dead time' so, as an economics graduate, startup entrepreneur, and NGO founder, he also spent the summer months in Central America working as a farmer to reflect and gain "an even more differentiated perspective of people, lenses, and lifestyles."

Despite being so young, Nader is already thinking about his legacy and wants to have "some sort of impact, some sort of lasting name that is there because you've built a life around purpose and people." With this in mind, he left the banking sector to join Dubai Tourism and establish a new strategic partnership division, and later, an advanced analytics division.

He found that his previous start-up experience enabled him to give good advice, as "a big chunk of the focus, there was to help the Dubai Future Foundation, where he later moved to, to set up what is now the Dubai Future District Fund." As part of the investment committee, he invested heavily in start-ups and firmly believes that they offer "opportunities for people to take their passions into projects, drive them to reality, and make life better for people around them." He has more recently moved into the Dubai Future District Fund to fully focus his time on precisely that motive.

Trust

Like many successful people, Nader is prone to experiencing imposter syndrome, particularly when he compares himself to "sectoral and functional experts." He relies on the encouragement of his network to overcome these insecurities, explaining how it can only "take that one person, and it doesn't come overnight, or in the first week, it sometimes takes a year for one person to turn around the day."

Regardless of his fears, it's his natural ability to create and maintain solid relationships that have enabled his great success. A natural conversationalist, he considers himself an expert in inspiring trust and being able to create a dialogue with anyone. Through this desire to connect, he feels grateful to have been given the opportunity to spend time with some "amazing organisations that attract a lot of really bright, driven, motivated individuals."

Nader remains grateful for his experiences, particularly as an undergraduate and military recruit, as they encouraged him to develop the ability to form relationships based on authenticity and trust. These shared experiences of "coming together" are something he compares to "connective tissue, it never fades." Something that's also helped when he's felt "like an outsider", is having very caring parents, which has given him the courage to face his fears head on. When he was younger, he developed arachnophobia, so he went into a cave with the largest tarantulas in the world in shorts and sandals just to overcome that fear. He believes that instead of running away from fear, it's important to embrace it and, in business, try to "make the team look at it as more of a challenge."

The 5-Year Plan

For Nader, having a 5-year plan to organise his goals is absolutely crucial. "When you're involved with so many different things at one time and an opportunity comes your way, it's really disruptive if you don't have a 5-year plan." As a reference point, it allows Nader to assess immediately whether a project is worth his time in the long term and if he can "reap enough benefits out of it."

Inspired by many people across business and life, Nader specifically cites Steve Jobs and Mahatma Gandhi as his main influences. The former because "he created simplicity in a very complex environment", and the latter because he "stood for many people on what they believed in." Since he's more focused on "the tiny little bits and pieces of impact", he's not looking for the same level of global fame and notoriety, happy in the knowledge that it's the small acts that can change the world one day at a time.

NIKOS LAGOUSAKOS

Creative & Show Director, Choreographer

The Fighter

Nikos is someone I deeply love and respect. I first met him when he was in his teenage years, but I 'discovered' him a few years ago. He is a fighter, with strong values and high empathy for the people he loves. I admire him for always being open to discuss openly any subject and standing his ground for the things he strongly believes in.

"The universe gives you signals and through experience, instinct and sensitivity you are responsible to see them, acknowledge them and make your own choices."

As the youngest of four siblings, Nikos was born in Australia to "Greek immigrant parents." From his experience, "Greeks who live abroad tend to be more Greek than those living in Greece", and he suggests that people who leave their home country take their language, traditions and customs with them and cherish them when they are away from home.

Greece was never far away from his parents' thoughts and when he was about 7 years old, the family moved back to their home country. Even though, this ushered in a period of turmoil for Nikos as he was bullied for not speaking fluent Greek and having a "high, girly voice." Instead of letting it ruin his confidence, he "figured out what [his] strength was and what made [him]." Nikos discovered his "social spirit and attitude", and became quite active in the student council, representing his class to ensure that all were treated equally and with fairness.

At school, Nikos became a highly respected teenager advocating for his peers. Nevertheless, he still had obstacles to overcome, and when he told his Greek father that he wanted to be a dancer, the response was one of shock. Regardless of Nikos' father's traditional Greek outlook, he had brought up his children to "choose [their] own path in life." And, after a short but explosive argument, he rapidly had his father's support, and started taking dance classes.

As Nikos fell in love with dance, his hobby soon turned into a great passion. Whilst he hated being on stage, he loved "creating, inspiring people and being behind the scenes, masterminding, and being the conductor of movement." At 20-years-old, he went on to audition for "the most prestigious dance school in Greece, the State School of Dance, but was told after one year that he would never become a dancer. "I remember that it was the most crazy thing that someone could even dare to think that was entitled to crush my dreams at an age when I was just discovering life." His school boy sense of justice came into play, "I thought it was the most outrageous and rude thing to do, and I told them so."

So, he decided to pursue choreography, and went on to study in Amsterdam, which turned out to be the "biggest gift of [his] life because [he] could discover who [he] was as a person and an artist."

"If you make that extra effort,
life is going to smile at you - but
you need to smile first."

He went on to participate in the Olympic ceremony in Athens as part of the choreography team. This experience led him to many other exciting projects, including 10 Olympic scale Ceremonies. He has worked on numerous Opera productions in some of the most prestigious theatres and festivals in Europe and was the artistic director for a dance festival, held in the biggest park in Moscow, Russia. Two of the projects that are close to his heart, for different reasons, are Clusters of Light that was staged in Sharjah and was about the Prophet Muhammad and the Origins of Islam, and the opening ceremony of the first Islamic Arts Biennale in Saudi Arabia.

After having travelled all over the world for his creative endeavours, during which he conceived, directed or choreographed from large-scale spectacles to performing art pieces, he has recently returned to Greece to open his own creative studio to work on projects and "bring the know-how, the coordination and organisation of how to execute the creative part, and to work in peace." He aimed to create his own "hub" so that he was able to work in "good conditions" and get the very best out of his collaborators.

This sense of collaboration is crucial to Nikos, and he feels the most comfortable when he is surrounded by his team, by people he trusts, who he "knows can do their thing." He insists that he doesn't like to micromanage, but "likes things to happen in the right way."

He's reflective about destiny, having experienced love and loss and depression, Nikos believes in the Greek word μοίρα (moira) - fate. During a creative process of a personal piece, he started jotting down stories, anecdotes, and memories from childhood, and began to understand that "the universe gives you signals and through experience, instinct and sensitivity you are responsible to see them, acknowledge them and make your own choices."

For Nikos, the field of performing arts and entertainment, is a series of lows and highs, beauty and friction. "We could work on just one show for a whole year, or maybe six months, and forget the bad things as we move onto the next project." He wants to do things differently by analysing what he did well, and was not done so well. He is keen to work with the right people, and create the proper conditions. "I like to inspire people, I like to feel secure, and to make others feel secure." Whether you have two performers or a hundred, my personal goal as a team leader, or director is to develop a positive energy and atmosphere."

Nikos has been on a long journey of emotion and learning and suggests that experience has taught him that if "you make that extra effort, life is going to smile at you - but you need to smile first."

NOHA HEFNY

Founder - The People of Impact | Top 100 Women in Social Enterprise 2021 | Asia's 100 Women Power Leaders 2022

The Purpose Driven

I met Noha a few years ago when she was still working with PepsiCo, and I was working with Facebook. We had connected to discuss some options for a Women's event I was organising with Facebook. We met again when we were both working together as part of the Unstereotype Alliance convened by UN Women, which Noha was chairing in the UAE. Since then, we found we have many things in common, one of which is our values and our purpose-driven approach to life. Noha was one of the people I reached out to, when I decided to move out of the corporate life and become a 360 degrees entrepreneur.

"Everything that I have done throughout my life, whether personally or professionally, has been completing pieces of a bigger puzzle - my purpose."

Noha Hefny is the visionary behind several social ventures she started on her own or with others, she is the founder of People of Impact, and previously the co-founder of 'She is Arab', a platform to address the under-representation of women in leadership, co-founder of Lit-Creative, a marketing agency. She is also a senior consultant at UN women, a co-author of three books, a global ambassador for women's rights, a multi-award winner and a board member. It's clear that all these pieces make up the "bigger puzzle" of her purpose, which is championing and driving women and youth leadership, wellbeing and advancement.

A Global Identity

Born into a family of diplomats that travelled all over the world, Noha attributes these early experiences to her subsequent career path and humanitarian ventures, believing that nothing is a coincidence.

Having been born in New Zealand, she lived in 7 other countries, including Switzerland, Ethiopia, Tunisia, Algeria, Sudan and Norway. After receiving a BA in Political Science with a specialization in International Relations, she began her career with the UN Refugee Agency (UNHCR), where she worked on a humanitarian mission facilitating the voluntary return of Eritrean refugees living in East Sudan back to their home country after years of conflict. For Noha, navigating different cultures has been an enriching experience, while "meeting amazing people" has enabled her to grow and develop into who she is today. From these experiences, she's developed a global identity with a strong sense of tolerance and inclusivity.

Even as a young girl, she was an overachiever. Her parents worked hard to achieve more, so Noha grew up with exceptional role models, an incredible work ethic, and a belief that "nothing is impossible, and you should see opportunities that come into your life as gifts to be leveraged and used for a good purpose and to serve."

> "You should see opportunities that come into your life as gifts to be leveraged and used for a good purpose and to serve."

Good Intentions

This "good purpose" has been an anchor for Noha's work in both the UN and as founder and CEO of People of Impact, a "global ecosystem and advisory firm for social good". She approaches any project or relationship with the intention to maximize impact and shared value for all, and believes this to be an uncompromising and core part of her identity because of how she was brought up.

This ethos and value system is also something she's determined to instil in her two boys. She's raised her family in a multicultural environment, ensuring that her sons are connected to their culture while maintaining a global mindset and being open to different people and cultures. Although she often asks herself whether she's "doing a good enough job", on reflection, she's mirrored her own parents, by enriching her boys' lives through education, role modelling behaviours, and nurturing their character through experiences. Her "good intention, impact and value mindset" is at the forefront of everything she does.

It's clear her parents' diplomatic careers have had a major influence on Noha's outlook, as she proudly possesses a "limitless ability to forgive and tolerate situations and be very diplomatic and tactful." She believes that "it is more important how you leave a relationship than how you start it, regardless of whether it's personal or professional." She's proud of the fact that she has never burned bridges even in some of the most challenging situations she had to confront.

"it is more important
how you leave a
relationship than how
you start it, regardless
of whether it's personal
or professional."

The Pieces of the Puzzle

During high school and university, Noha took on leadership roles in the Model United Nations programmes in her school and university, leading her to become the Secretary General of the Model United Nations Programme at the American International School in Cairo back in 1996-1997 and in college heading several councils in the same program. This journey continued when she was elected as part of the student council at college. After graduation, Noha made it to the UN High Commissioner for Refugees (UNHCR) as a volunteer, later being hired to join the organisation as a national and then an international Staff.

At 22 years of age, she was in a refugee camp in East Sudan and, one year later, in South Algeria. It not only broadened her attitude towards different cultures and people, but being given the opportunity to experience so much at such a young age encouraged her to develop resilience, perseverance, understanding, and the ability to manage issues in crisis. During a role, that required her to live and work in remote locations, she was able to rely on her natural agility, faith, determination and patience to carry her through.

She also consulted with UNESCO, where her role focused on education. She spent the next 10 years of her career working in the corporate sector with PepsiCo, developing her career from managing internal communications to founding and leading the corporate affairs department for the Middle East and Africa region, which dealt with all PR and communications, public affairs, and corporate social responsibility. Later on, she joined McKinsey & Company in a similar role but with a much broader geography, becoming the director of communications for Eastern Europe, the Middle East, and Africa, one of four global directors in the communications functions.

Those experiences in her career really shaped how Noha interacts and relates to others professionally. She developed a deep sense of humility, understanding that her background was one of extreme privilege, something that was not offered to many people. It has allowed her to be more accepting of different circumstances and adapt to new and unfamiliar situations with flexibility.

Her most recent "piece of the puzzle" has been as founder of 'People of Impact', an advisory firm and ecosystem working on advancing social impact and the SDGs, which she established in 2020.

With all her achievements, it's no surprise that Noha has been the recipient of many awards. Yet the one she's most proud of is the International Women's Day Euclid Network Top 100 Women in Social Enterprise. To be recognised on a global level was a formidable milestone for Noha as she completes the pieces of the puzzle.

Leading Like a Woman

For Noha, the value of authenticity is deep-rooted. She has no interest in fitting into a certain mould set by an organisation, family, friends, or even society. She is a free spirit in this world and will always remain so. Her innovative, disruptive, and creative nature leads her to new ventures, ideas that are out of the box, and she creates her own to show up in the world in a way that she believes in and that aligns to her values, not the other way around. It's this uncompromising attitude towards authenticity that she tries to instil in younger women, "that they can still succeed and demonstrate a new type of leadership by being themselves and pushing boundaries to innovate and succeed."

Having worked in 3 distinct sectors; the United Nations, the corporate world, and then as a social entrepreneur, Noha is aware that they all have individual expectations for leadership. Nevertheless, she believes that a good leader on all accounts is achieved through being "open to people, purpose and values-driven, inclusive, and most of all, authentic." Her commitment to authenticity means that she's transparent about how she feels, is herself with her team, which in turn sets her apart from the more typical and traditional forms of leadership.

"A good leader on all accounts is achieved through
being open to people, purpose and values-driven,
inclusive, and most of all, authentic."

Her leadership style has been successful in building very strong teams with a limited budget and resources. Even during rough periods when she was in situations where resources were limited, her signature human-centric approach, authenticity, transparency, sensitivity, and diplomacy ensured that she was able to maintain a solid and motivated team around her.

Like many modern entrepreneurs, Noha is a great believer in getting the most out of people by allowing them tobe their human selves, to show their vulnerability if need be. It could be because she is a female leader, but hiding emotions is not something she perceives as a strength. She also feels an innate drive to have some sort of lasting impact, to create value, and to best understand her strengths and weaknesses so that she can put her best foot forward when collaborating with others.

A defining moment

Travelling the globe has obviously left an indelible impression on Noha. "I think I am proud of every experience I have had, positive or negative. In every experience is a lesson, a chance for growth and expansion of the self." When she was living in Ethiopia as a child, she remembers that although she was only about 12 or 13 years old, she was conscious of the fact that she had a generally privileged existence. Yet, she was also painfully aware of the abject poverty that existed close by; right outside of her door, some people lived in slums with a few metal sheets for shelter, and only very basic resources with their children having no shoes and studying in the dark. Exposure to injustice at such an early age sparked something strong within Noha, and she began volunteering at charity events and taking on leadership roles in her school to help disadvantaged members of the community.

Leaders who have reached the height of success can often appear indestructible, so it's refreshing when individuals like Noha are happy to talk about their more vulnerable side. She speaks to general anxieties and worries, times when she felt physically unsafe during difficult situations on her travels in remote areas, as well as facing the inner turmoil of imposter syndrome when she first stepped into leadership. Particularly after pivoting into a competitive and fast-paced corporate environment, "controlling the flow, and setting her agenda and that of her function instead of following a set agenda creates its own set of doubts in the beginning until one can adapt."

However, Noha is not defined by moments of self-doubt, fear, and anxiety; she is defined by her determination, diplomacy, strategic mind, innovative spirit, one of kindness, empathy, and tolerance. Her ability to think globally while acting locally makes her a promoter of peace, a mediator who can bring people to the table, an impact creator in every sense of the word, and it's these experiences that have moulded her into a true humanitarian and leader with a distinct sense of justice and purpose and an ability to identify and support those most in need and anyone she has the power to influence or inspire.

"In every experience is a
lesson, a chance for growth
and expansion of the self."

NOOR SWEID

Founder and Managing Partner at Global Ventures

The No-Nonsense

When I arrived at Noor's office for the interview, I was aware that I needed to be punctual, concise, and prepared for a straightforward discussion. We had met a few times before, most of our encounters were in a professional setting. Noor has a mindset of a protagonist and is a confident communicator. While she is approachable, she sets boundaries and sticks to them. She has a good sense of humour, and I love that, and knows when to share a story or a laugh. To sum it up, Noor embodies what I refer to as a visible and confident protagonist.

At the time of this book's publication, Noor Sweid is notably featured as one of the judges on the Shark Tank Dubai TV series, joining a panel of esteemed business professionals.

"Everything is a blessing in disguise,
and the meaning of life really stems
from the acknowledgment of human
need versus human desire."

For Noor Sweid, who runs a venture capital firm that invests in the Middle East, Africa and Pakistan, backing entrepreneurs in sectors such as healthcare, education, food or financial services are priorities because the solutions they are building serve considerable underserved and unserved markets who need access to healthcare, schooling, learning, food and financial services and have long been excluded from formal institutions.

Considering the path less travelled the most interesting, she describes herself as an "entrepreneur 95% of the time and an investor 5% of the time." It's the road that challenges you to explore new parts of yourself, and pushes you to grow and explore your creativity. Most importantly, it's the one that pushes you to bring the best version of yourself to the table.

Finance for Pharma

Early in her career, Noor discovered the impact that businesses, and innovation, could have on communities, individuals, and nations worldwide – and wanted to be part of the solution. The motives were, first and foremost, personal. After graduating with a BS in Economics and Finance, she pursued a career in biotech and pharmaceutical consulting. It was her experience with a rigid, one-size-fits-all healthcare system that drove her to seek alternatives and when she didn't find any, she built one – but more on that later. In the short term, however, she was eager to work with companies focused on innovation in cellular and biological processes to combat diseases, which motivated an early career in biotechnology. Although her dream was to be an investment banker, fate sent her in an entirely different direction.

A Working Mum

"I learned early on that work-life balance is a myth, and that it is best to seek life balance" or in other words, instead of trying to balance work and home, it is better to integrate them. Noor's daily routine starts with an early wake-up call, a meditation session followed by a morning coffee, and then waking the kids, usually with some jazz music. They have breakfast together, she drops them off at school, then goes to the gym. So, like many working mothers, by the time she reaches the office, she already achieved quite a lot before arriving for work. At 4.30pm, she leaves the office to spend time with her kid. It's a well-considered system that works. Noor makes a point of not working between the hours of 4:30-8pm so that she can prioritise spending as much time as possible with her family. Once her children are in bed at 8pm, Noor will often continue to work until 11.30pm or later. The time difference between Dubai and the US bodes well for her in that regard. "It's about having a perspective on life." She realises that everything is a blessing in disguise, and the meaning of life really stems from the acknowledgment of human need versus human desire.

The Business of Yoga

"I don't believe in retirement; I believe in sabbaticals." Her future seems mapped out for at least the next 10 years, before she could potentially take a short break. Noor believes that when the time is right, the opportunity will present itself. For example, 20 years ago, she wouldn't have imagined running a venture capital firm, but she finds the role creative, satisfying, and rewarding in many ways.

When Noor moved back to the UAE in 2005, she joined her father's interior contracting firm Depa for what was initially supposed to be a 3-week reorganization project. A few years later, the company had grown from $60 million in revenues to $600 million, and from 6 countries to 22. She then took Depa to the public markets, making her the first-ever Arab woman to lead an IPO in the region. To offset the stress of the job, Noor typically resorts to a yoga practice. It was always her go-to outlet for stress, but was surprised with the lack of studios in Dubai, which she saw as an opportunity to build one. Within 4 years of her first studio opening, the business had expanded to several locations, 72

teachers, and thousands of students each month.

She eventually sold the business to a private equity firm. Her experience as an entrepreneur taught her a valuable lesson: that, in some ways, it is much harder to build a business from scratch than to run an existing billion-dollar company. A lesson that defined her next career move: supporting and enabling entrepreneurs.

Creating Impact

In 2016, she became CIO of the Dubai Future Foundation, working with the government to create investment strategies for a venture ecosystem with the aim of transforming Dubai from a tourist destination to an innovation hub. In 2017, she left to start her venture capital firm, Global Ventures, which has invested in 60 companies across the Middle East and Africa, from Nigeria and Kenya to Saudi Arabia and Pakistan.

Noor is deeply passionate about generating opportunities to boost employment and "build an alternate narrative for the region in terms of success stories." And with an impressive portfolio of companies under her belt, her firm has the

capacity to affect millions of people across the Middle East and Africa through technology and innovation.

"Through our portfolio of companies, over 57 million people have been financially included, and over 6.8 million people now have access to health care. Our companies have created over 10,000 jobs, and 32% of our founders and CCPs are female. We measure these things because they're important."

The Gender Gap

When discussing equality and inclusion, Noor shares that much of the global trends on insufficient funding for female founders are reflected in the region where she operates. She is proud, however, that her company's portfolio boasts over 30% of female founders or co-founders. Her belief is that across all barometers, a high level of involvement from women in leadership positions is fundamental to a company's performance from a financial and social impact perspective.

While she believes that the challenge of under-representation is largely systemic, Noor has taken active steps in trying to empower women in the ecosystem by participating in regional female-focused conferences, mentoring female founders, facilitating introductions and hosting dedicated events. Guided by the belief that what gets measured gets managed, her company carefully measures female participation in leadership positions across the portfolio of start-ups.

Joining the Dots

Having been based in Dubai for a while now, Noor praises the UAE in terms of its safety and its business and investment prospects. Its geographical location, at the intersection of East and West, makes it an ideal place for business-building, and its leadership has long fostered a culture of innovation and entrepreneurship. As an entrepreneur herself, emerging markets are precisely where she wants to focus her intentions, energy, talent, and capital in the hopes of paying it forward and shifting established narratives.

RAMEZ T. SHEHADI

President & Chief Growth Officer - REEF

The Navigator

Ramez's affinity for Stoicism and Greek Zorbas, is particularly captivating, and speaks to my Greek heart. Amidst the COVID-19 crisis, when we were both working at Facebook, his leadership focused on supporting our team while adeptly managing business concerns. Ramez's mentoring, often unintentionally impactful, balances tough discussions with genuine empathy and care. His visionary outlook, readiness to support peers, and generous nature make him an exceptional figure. His navigation of change, akin to charting new courses in sailing, reflects his love for the sea and his ability to guide others through transformation.

Born in Lebanon and raised in Saudi Arabia, where his father served as an executive at Saudi Aramco (the national oil company of Saudi Arabia), Ramez holds very fond memories of his early years growing up as an "Aramco Brat". At age 14, since the schooling system provided by Aramco only reached the 9th grade for expats and civil war raged in Lebanon, his parents decided that he was to finish off his secondary education in the US at a college preparatory boarding school in New York called 'The Stony Brook School'. This was to be the first of many deeply impactful experiences in his life, each building on the other, galvanizing values, reinforcing learnings, testing resilience, and confirming support networks in family, faith and friends.

This journey began with a simple, yet profound, directive from his father as he departed from dropping him off at boarding school, "Ramez, you have all that you need… now you have to be a man."

An accomplished and agile Chief Executive with over 25 years of experience as a senior leader, Ramez is a seasoned board member and digital transformation specialist, managing and advising diverse institutions varying in complexity and size globally. A proficient "builder" of companies, products, platforms, and solutions, he possesses the unique ability to unite fragmented elements, galvanize teams, and drive impactful growth. With an unwavering focus and an inclusive vision, he leads the way in constructing and expanding business models, navigating through often-uncharted territories, and driving progress to an intentional and profitable conclusion. Responsible for vast territories and markets and having built successful businesses from the ground up, he has strong interpersonal skills and is exceptional at forming and developing cohesive, high-performing teams driven to achieve results. He is a charismatic and engaging leader who understands the intricacies of leading teams across multi-regional and cultural backgrounds, and is adept at quickly assessing situations and developing and implementing growth and/or redirection strategies. Ramez is actively involved in community leadership initiatives, having designed, built, and led various social responsibility programs regionally and globally. He is also a sought-after voice on international media platforms, including the Financial Times, the Guardian, Forbes, Gulf News, Arab News, Arabian Business, WEF GITR, L'Orient, Atlantic Council, The Economist and CNN, among others.

The Professional Journey

From a very young age, Ramez had hoped to one day become a surgeon, drawn by a deep curiosity in how things worked, and how to make them better. Although medical school wasn't in his future, engineering was, earning his first degree in Mechanical Engineering from Rutgers University.

As a young engineer, Ramez started off at Stone & Webster, once one of the world's engineering giants that offered design, construction, environmental and engineering services to build power and petrochemical plants, refineries, and infrastructure projects for clients all around the world. After spending time on large refinery upgrade programs in the Middle East, it became clear that his true calling lay elsewhere and with more business exposure.

It was at the University of Toronto, while earning a Masters of Applied Science degree in Industrial Engineering, that Ramez was invited to join a globally leading think tank in the field of non-parametric linear programming named, The Centre for Management of Technology & Entrepreneurship (CMTE). And it was at the CMTE that the connection between engineering and business first became clear. It was this insight that ultimately propelled him into the world of business and technology strategy consulting, where his interests and capabilities in engineering, innovation, and problem solving all came together in one profession. Over the next 25 years, Ramez came in and out of the consulting industry three times oscillating between advising,

> "Lead by influence. Get teams to deliver not because they are told, but because they come to believe it's the right thing to do."

operating, and building businesses and capabilities in both the public and private sectors around the world.

In the late 90's, just as the first dot.com bubble ballooned, Ramez was learning the consulting craft at Kearney (formerly A.T.Kearney), one of the original global management consulting firms specialized in strategic operations and large transformations for the Fortune Global 500. Soon, he too succumbed to the "irrational exuberance" of the time, as the Chairman of the US Federal Reserve, Allen Greenspan, described the markets' excitement over tech innovation coming out of the Silicon Valley, and he left to stand-up eBreviate.com in San Francisco. As head of product development and engineering, he helped eBreviate become a global B2B eSourcing unicorn serving Fortune 500 clients through a suite of auctions, supplier identification and spending management tools.

When the dot.com bubble burst, neither an IPO nor a sale of eBreviate were in the books, but another round in consulting was! In 2001, he joined the Digital Business & Technology Practice of Strategy& (formerly Booz & Company), a global management consulting firm noteable for having developed the essential concepts of 'human capital', 'product life cycle', 'supply chain management', 'smart customization', 'organizational DNA', among many others. He eventually became a partner and practice leader in the firm, and a member of its Middle East management team. Ramez co-created and globally co-managed Booz Digital, one of the earliest venture-building platforms in the consulting industry worldwide – pushing boundaries to deliver tangible and measurable outcomes for clients. He reflects, "At some point, I got bored with traditional consulting – only putting ideas down on paper – and so we built a global corporate-foundry to innovate with and for our clients; combining the power of cutting edge design, engineering, advertising and consulting industries, we turned ideas into viable new products, services, businesses." In 2014, Ramez rejoined Booz Allen Hamilton, among the oldest of the global business and technology consulting firms with deep expertise in analytics, digital, engineering, and cyber to help public (civil and defense) and private organizations transform, as a senior partner and managing director tasked with re-establishing a leading

international strategy consulting capability after it has shed that capability in the formation of Booz & Company back in 2008.

Another pivot to industry occurred 2018, when Ramez joined Meta (formerly Facebook) as its MENA Managing Director to lead iconic platforms like Facebook, Instagram,WhatsApp, Messenger, Workplace, and Oculus. He played a pivotal role in the digital revolution of the region through his vision, aptly named 'Yalla' ("Let's Go!" in Arabic), to amplify the impact of a mobile-first philosophy, giving millions of people and institutions a voice and the means to build meaningful social and commercial communities. He fondly reflects, "it was very different at Meta. I learned how to 'lead by influence' – getting teams to deliver not because they are told, but because they come to believe it's the right thing to do, while understanding their part in something much greater than themselves. I learned the power of 'resourcefulness'." By the start of 2022, Ramez was recruited to serve as President and Global Chief Growth Officer of REEF, a groundbreaking technology platform based in Miami. With backing from Mubadala and SoftBank, REEF transformed communities into vibrant hubs, offering a wide range of goods, services, and experiences, by emphasizing "proximity as a service". In his role, Ramez helped reshape the way people live within their communities, focusing on personalization, convenience, and speed of services.

<blockquote>
"'Success is not final, failure is not fatal; but it is the courage to continue [that matters most]' as Churchill once said. Understanding this, has taught me to maintain my ballast amidst prevailing storms both seen and unseen, to rest, recharge and refocus in fair weather, and to have the energy to overcome the most dangerous of notions that 'this is just the way things are' and 'this is how we've always done it'."
</blockquote>

Today, Ramez is amidst yet another pivot filled with new learnings, impact and relevance to the digital future and the global communities affected by it. Beyond his professional accomplishments, he remains a passionate advocate for social responsibility and diversity. He takes active roles in community leadership and governance initiatives, working tirelessly to drive positive change on crucial issues like women's empowerment, sustainability, and social entrepreneurship.

When asked about the clear theme of building and creating throughout his career, whether businesses, institutional capabilities, teams or cultures, he simply shares a sentiment from the author of "Good to Great", Jim Collins, "there is something special about the act of bringing people, needs, opportunities together and about making one plus one equaling three. Its about knowing that you've had a hand in creating something of intrinsic excellence that makes a contribution, that leaves a mark, that time has been well spent and that it mattered… not only does your work move toward greatness, but so does your life."

Philosophy

Ramez draws significant inspiration from Stoic philosophy. He believes in using all experiences - difficult or smooth alike - as opportunities for introspection and learning, asking himself, "What can be gained or learned from this?" Authenticity is also a core value for him; he emphasizes the importance of being true to himself in every aspect of life, be it professional, personal, or social. "With time, I learned to shed my masks - I try to be myself no matter the occasion or the audience", he asserts. The diverse experiences and relationships he's cultivated throughout his life have been instrumental in shaping his genuine self. He feels fortunate for these life experiences, from experiencing his heritage to driving global technological innovations, and building a family and lifelong friendships.

In April of 2018, Ramez embarked on a transformative 30-day, 470 km hike on an ancient trail across Lebanon, traversing 75 villages at various mountain elevations from the country's southern to its northern tip with various people from Lebanon, the region and around the world. The route was lined with ancient monuments and reminders of past and present conflicts, offered breathtaking natural beauty and a poignant view across Lebanon's complex history. This journey in nature also helped distill a few key lessons that he shares:

Ups & Downs Are Guaranteed

Life will present you with hills and mountains, valleys and ravines, plateaus and soft fields literally and figuratively... the ascents and descents can be much harder than you've ever imagined or easier than you expected; the journey can be complicated by injury, fear, failing gear, bad weather, the natural wildness of the flora and fauna or made easy by fair weather, clear and flat passage, and the strength of good nutrition, healthy mind and body. At times you may find yourself well prepared and others not. You will succeed and you will fail – but your successes will not be final and your failures will not be fatal! Recharge when you can, be agile and always adapt. When the goals or challenges are daunting, don't give up – keep moving... take one step at a time until you reach the destination at hand... And amidst this, be generously available to support others as invariably you'll need others to be there for you as you navigate the ups and downs.

Set Your Own Pace

On life's trail, some are faster and stronger than you, smarter and with more endurance than you, more experienced and insightful than you; but also some slower and weaker, with less resilience, sense or capability than you... And you may find yourself unconsciously keeping a pace with a group that erodes your sense of purpose, makes you doubt yourself or your principals... Raise your head up from only looking immediately ahead of you and only at what others around you are doing ... "Comparison is the thief of joy"... be true to your authentic self and set your own pace – it's your adventure; live your own experience, not someone else's... look up and see life around you, appreciate where you came from, consider the path you are on and the destination you've chosen and adjust, trim, refocus.

Navigate From A Reference

'The longitude problem' was among the most difficult of scientific dilemmas for centuries. Lacking the ability to measure their longitude, sailors throughout the ages of exploration had been practically lost at sea as soon as they lost sight of land. While the scientific establishment of Europe – from Galileo to Newton – had mapped the heavens in its pursuit of a celestial answer, one man, John Harrison, imagined a mechanical solution – a clock that would keep precise time at sea and enable the mariner to always know what time it was at an agreed-upon zero-meridian, as well as aboard the ship (by setting the local clock to noon when the sun was directly overhead). The two clock times would then enable the conversion of the hour difference into a geographical east-west separation.

Family, faith and values can be your meridian. Explore and navigate the adventures ahead of you, with a confidence and trust in your reference.

Plant Trees Along the Way

Planting a tree is an investment that yields multiple returns… it shelters from the elements and predators, holds the soil and its nutrients, provides warmth, bares food, enables building and travel, and spawns new life around it… but it takes time, attention, requires resources, and frequent care and pruning to help make it grow strong and to bear fruit.

If not careful, it's easy to get trapped in the world of instant clicks of gratification, solving for the immediate at the expense of the meaningful, surrendering what we know to be right for what feels good, to chase what we want, not what we need. In this world, filled with extremes, you are among the privileged, gifted with opportunities beyond the reach of many. Use what is available to you intelligently, with all your facilities - plant trees and invest in what will grow beyond you.

SALLYANN DELLA CASA

CEO & Chief Identity Hacker - GLEAC

The Privileged

Driven, talented and multifaceted, Sallyann has high expectations from everyone around her, but mostly from herself. Yet at the same time, she sees the value of being open to "apologise", or saying "I don't know", and "I really appreciate it." Her business philosophy is a new kind of ideology where, instead of "defensive blame and ego nonsense, there is a starting point of humility."

When Sallyann is not running her network, GLEAC, an SaaS platform and community of over 500 world-leading experts helping people innovate and strive, she could perhaps be found in a bookshop. Reading 5 books at a time, she has a hunger for knowledge, and sharing it with those who will listen.

Growing up in a "church going family" that also celebrates Eid because of her grandfather, and Hinduism because of her father, it's clear that Sally Ann's world view is as eclectic as her bookshelf. Coming from a Caribbean Island with 1.3 million inhabitants, Sallyann was educated in Toronto and the US, whilst also spending some of her formative years in Switzerland.

> "I see the value of being open to apologise, or saying I don't know, and I really appreciate it."

Throughout her upbringing, she developed a strong academic identity. However, she reflects on how her motivation to learn was perhaps driven by not feeling as though she were taken seriously, and feeling like she needed to prove to her family that she was more than just a pretty face. Indeed, Sallyann exceeded everyone's expectations and, by the age of 21, she already had 5 degrees to her name.

Growing up in the Caribbean developed her world-view, and she considers the "community feel" of Trinidad and Tobago a beautiful gift during her upbringing. Every Friday evening, different families would gather, and she recalls having friends in their 50s and 60s when she was only 16, something "that has to do with the island mentality - there were no barriers of age or race." She also remembers how they'd drink with their parents, "alcohol at 13 was OK, and so in that respect it was very European."

It's this deeply ingrained sense of community that has really paved the way for Sally Ann's venture, GLEAC, a mentorship platform with a "community of industry experts showing you all those blind spots and hidden areas, extending a hand, and helping you on your journey." Giving users access to a network of experts from different ages, races, and places in the world, it's a virtual community that makes wisdom available for people to learn and network faster. Yet, she's most proud of the fact that her tech company is made up of 40% women, spanning over 9 countries.

Interestingly, Sallyann suggests that "when you build technology, it's actually formed from many parts of who you are as a person" and the concept of GLEAC was born from her own ability to "learn anything rapidly, and teach it back to you the same day." With an impressive ability to synthesise huge amounts of complex information, and relay it to others in a way they will understand, her skills are high in demand. As just one example, Sallyann was recently invited to Istanbul to give a talk on blockchain systems to a prolific bank. Whilst her initial knowledge of the subject was limited, she used her "vertical" learning agility to digest five courses on the topic over a weekend. Becoming an expert on Merkle Trees, a fundamental component of blockchains, allowing for efficient and secure verification of large data structures, she was then able to give an informative and enriching lecture on the subject with confidence.

For Sallyann, her issue has typically been people not seeing her for who she really is, something that GLEAC seeks to rectify. She suggests that the platform "allows people who are not normally seen,

"When you build technology, it's actually formed from many parts of who you are as a person."

to be able to showcase themselves and display their emotional IQ, creative thinking, or communication skills. Developing GLEAC can be seen as a response to her own personal struggle in life, "of being seen for the things that are not at the surface." So, creating this network has been a deeply personal mission for Sallyann, who believes that it is the "best parts of us that are never seen, and the best parts of us are what make us authentically ourselves."

As one of only 4% of women globally with a patent-pending method and algorithm for measuring soft skills, Sallyann also holds a Master's in Organisational Behaviour from Harvard, and a doctorate in Law from St Thomas University, Miami. Nevertheless, she describes her greatest achievement as publishing her first book in 2016. "I went into the world's largest bookstore and there, on the shelf next to the likes of Robin Sharma and Tony Robbins, was my book. It was that moment I said to myself: 'This is the most successful I've ever been in my life'. The feeling of going from the nerdy kid who read all these books to suddenly having my own book, sitting in the bookstore." For Sallyann, success has little to do with material goods, status or titles, "it's an internal thing".

Despite being a uniquely accomplished individual, Sallyann is still refreshingly human and approachable. She is the type who smiles at complete strangers, "as a simple act of kindness", and refuses to follow the purely transactional path many adopt in this fast-changing and competitive world. "I think the reason I connect so well with others is that people actually feel that vulnerability with me, and they feel that connect, even though the ornaments of, say, my job title, or what they see on social media might look impressive, I am not afraid to show my scars, questions and doubts. And I share that publicly."

She explains that she uses her vulnerability to make bridges and connect with other people because she can say out loud what many might be thinking. For Sallyann, vulnerability is a strength because she is competent in what she does. Citing the 'pratfall effect' in social psychology, she believes that because she delivers, she can afford that level of vulnerability.

Sallyann currently has 20 employees and during the onboarding session with her teams, she makes a point of saying that she feels privileged to be with them on their journey. She regards all employees as alumni of GLEAC, and is happy to have "created a stepping stone for the next version of whom [they] will become." However, she is not afraid to have "crucial conversations and deal with discomfort while they're learning who they will become… How people are growing, and the quality of their questions, is what allows people to thrive in my organisation." It's not possible to hide in a corner at GLEAC, the pace of the organisation is just too fast.

For now, Sally is starting a project called 'Restart' where they engage with pre-millennials who are changing careers. "We are bringing in 50-year-olds who are asking: 'What do I do now?' With this new project, we will be able to bridge that gap." Quite rightly, she believes there's a generation of well-educated people, who have had super powerful jobs and are trying to figure it out all over again, so she will be introducing them, for example, to emerging technologies, Web 3.0 and Green skills. Exciting stuff, so watch this space.

"How people are growing, and the quality
of their questions, is what allows people
to thrive in my organisation."

SHARON NISHI

Chair and Managing Director - GM Egypt and North Africa

The Purpose Driven

Through a mutual acquaintance, I had the pleasure of meeting Sharon over coffee, where we discussed a wide range of topics from business to personal aspirations. At the time, she was preparing to take on the role of Managing Director for Egypt and North Africa, making her one of the few female Managing Directors at GM and in the Auto industry worldwide.

Sharon was thrilled about her new position and the opportunities it presented. I found Sharon to be an exceptional individual both in a professional and personal capacity - fearless and forward-thinking.

"I don't know if I could have come home without a good grade from school. It was important to be number one."

Uniquely dedicated, Sharon Nishi has been working for the same company for 36 years and married to the same man for 30. However, her life hasn't always been so stable - something that she considers a blessing looking back. Having explored 66 countries and chosen to settle in four over the years, she's managed to carve herself an exciting global career.

Japan to Canada

When Sharon looks back on her childhood, there's a deep sense of appreciation for the tools her parents gave her to thrive. Her father was a commercial fisherman, and she believes that watching him run his own business, being responsible for his own income, and being malleable to changes in weather and seasons instilled in her an entrepreneurial spirit from the offset. Coming from a modest background with Japanese heritage, she's proud to be "a third generation Japanese Canadian, meaning we trace our history in Canada back 3 generations." Sharon grew up in Vancouver with very high expectations from her parents; hard work, perseverance, and a good education were the pillars of her upbringing. Although her parents made sure their daughters assimilated well into Canadian culture, they also recognised the value of remaining close to their Japanese culture, and Sharon grew up speaking Japanese as her primary language.

After working hard at school all week to maintain perfect grades, Sharon would then spend Saturday mornings at a Japanese school. As a child, she resented being in class at a time when her peers were able to relax, play, and socialise. But as an adult, she looks back on this time with endless gratitude, knowing that the mindset, language, and culture have been a true asset.

She was raised in a very multicultural environment. With friends with roots from China, Italy, and India, she developed a wanderlust that she's proud to say

"Relationships matter, and there is no replacement for hard work".

she has well and truly fulfilled. More importantly, it has given her the ability to create connections with all sorts of people, and she puts great emphasis on the importance of networking and relationships in both personal and professional endeavours.

Climbing the Ladder

After graduating with a Degree in Business, she had an interview for General Motors. Despite not really knowing much about cars, there were a number of company behaviours that really caught her attention as a young graduate entering the workforce. The company was actively pushing to hire more women in 1986, a time when it wasn't such a global directive. There were also many opportunities for global assignments. Yet, it was the process of the second round of interviews that really impressed her, via a series of tests and workshops that really investigated the strengths and weaknesses of the candidates. She became sure that this was a company that would nurture young talent, and nurture her it certainly did, as 36 years later she's still working with GM in Cairo.

Making her start in sales, she provided information about strategies, objectives, and business consulting to dealers, who were mostly middle-aged businessmen. An intimidating position for a young woman in her early 20s to be in, establishing herself within a male-oriented environment became an invaluable experience in developing strong leadership skills. Her incredible work ethic was able to win over any dealers unsure about her youth and gender, and many long hours in the office, sometimes 7 days a week, demonstrated her support and commitment to the role.

She quickly moved up the career ladder into a more strategic role at the head office. Every 2 or 3 years, employees move around internally, learning new roles and skills, having new experiences, and being constantly challenged while taking a bigger view of the company. "I never said no to a change in a job. Even if they were not progressing up, but more across, it gave me the experience I needed and was a good foundation for what I needed to do down the road."

A Milestone

A real turning point for her was her first international assignment, being provided the opportunity to become

AL MOT RS

the Regional Marketing Manager for the Asia Pacific region in Singapore. Then, when the operation moved from Singapore to Shanghai, Sharon ran the sales operations and network development, utilising her early experience with the dealers to inform her approach. Over 4 years, she diversified her skill set and rolled out workshops and training programmes across Asia, from China to South East Asia and India, to develop the young talent across the region. Her dream of working and experiencing many countries was finally realised, but it didn't stop there.

She later became Director for Sales and Marketing in Latin America, Africa, and the Middle East. And with GM's post-bankruptcy restructuring, Sharon found herself back in Shanghai, China heading Marketing for International Operations, continuing her passion for global business and transforming marketing to a more digital customer-centric approach with responsibilities spanning 4 continents.

The Future is Female

At 58 years old, Sharon considers herself to be at "the tail end" of her career, but her work ethic doesn't show any signs of slowing down as GM's new Managing Director of Egypt and North Africa. It's clear that Sharon loves what she does, and work is where she feels the greatest sense of accomplishment.

Mentorship is crucial to Sharon. It's something that she valued immensely as a young graduate and is now something she pays forward regularly as a seasoned executive. However, she's often slightly dismayed that men reach out for mentoring opportunities far more often than young women. She doesn't suggest a reason for this, but she does stress the importance of mentorship for all in building a network and growing fruitful relationships.

It is her appreciation for others that really stands out, from acknowledging her husband, who has been "an incredible support system... a real trusted advisor, tutor, and just an incredible spouse", to championing General Motors CEO Mary Barra. Since the start of her career, she has been very conscious of her position as a woman in business, and she's really excited by GM's future with a female CEO at the helm transforming her company to a more sustainable and environmentally friendly business model, with a mission to be carbon-neutral by 2040.

Sharon too shares that same aspiration of making the world a better place by helping transform the organisation she has spent her working life into a "zero crashes, zero emissions, zero congestion" car manufacturer.

Her values boil down to basically two things; "relationships matter, and there is no replacement for hard work". She also quotes Madeleine Albright, stating that "there is a special place in hell for women who don't help other women." With lifelong experience in the corporate world, she's witnessed many women who have been reluctant to help each other, and believes that might have something to do with their hesitant attitude towards mentorship. Looking forward, she wants to see a collective movement among women in business where they stop seeing each other as competitors and start seeing each other as potential collaborators.

SONIA TRIGUEROS

Founder and Director - NIVD World

The Intelligent

Sonia's personality immediately strikes you as warm and welcoming, but it's her intelligence and resilience that truly leave you awestruck. When we first met, her vibrant energy and dedication to positively impacting others was instantly palpable. We connected so effortlessly that it felt like meeting a long-lost friend. I left our conversation feeling energized and fortunate to have formed a new friendship with someone as remarkable as Sonia.

At school, Sonia was often left feeling insecure about her learning capabilities. Although it was known of the existence of different learning styles, she was caught between an innate curiosity for science and an inability to recall information in a classroom setting. It was the start of an uphill battle, one that was won through sheer passion and determination, and now Sonia holds an Associated Professor position at Barcelona University, a postdoctoral research degree in molecular biology from Harvard University and several academic research positions at the University of Oxford.

Although she admits that it was difficult and "took longer than normal people", she discovered that her strength was "in her visual memory". And now, as a founder and former co-director of the Oxford Martin Programme on Nanotechnology, she is at the forefront of ground-breaking research, asking challenging questions like "is a vaccine for cancer possible?"

> "When I was a child, our education system put
> me in the category of non-intelligent person."

Biology to Physics

A two-year contract at the University of Oxford lasted seventeen years, and it was there that she first discovered 'nanotechnology' and shifted from biology into physics. She describes the move from one discipline to another as disorienting because they "speak completely different languages", but she was left awestruck at the ability to see DNA at the atomic level under their microscopes and found a passion that drove her to stick around for ten years. Eventually finding her equilibrium state at the Biophysics sub department, she "became the interface between biology and the physics of the cell." Working with a team of physicists, engineers, and chemists, they began research into ways cancer could be treated at early stages using emerging new nanomaterials and their new properties at the nano level (a nanometre is a thousandth of a thousandth of a millimetre).

Working at the Nano level raised issues. She learned that by making materials so small, they found new properties that completely changed them. The problem for Sonia was how she was going to study things when she didn't know how they behaved, "nothing you knew could be applied."

Rather than hindering her efforts, this space for innovation and experimentation excited her curious mind, "it was like another scenario of innovating, creating new things, and changing things. I started designing new projects." Sonia then met James Martin, a physicist and entrepreneur who set up the Oxford Martin School within Oxford University, and together they founded the first Institute of Nanomedicine in Oxford.

In her research, Sonia was concerned that approximately only around 3% of medicine reaches its target. For something like a painkiller, this doesn't matter as long as the pain goes away quickly enough. But with chemotherapy, only 3% gets to the tumour, the rest just produces nasty side effects in the body. With nanotechnology, Sonia invented a way to specifically target the cancerous cells, but she found that by the time cancer had been diagnosed, and a tumour detected, it was always too late.

Frustrated with the diagnostic system, she set up her own company during the COVID lockdown. She knew the science but had "no idea about business", so she founded NIVD in November 2021 and formed an executive team between herself and co-founder Xavier Anglada.

Now, Sonia's company is developing pre-symptomatic diagnostic technology, with the aim of training Nano-sensors to detect human disease as easily as possible. An early example of personalised medicine and the future of patient care as we know it. She has already received tempting offers from buyers to acquire the company, but she insists, "that

"I just want to be happy, when I'm happy, I'm creative, and innovative and that is the Sonia I like to be."

is not my aim." Perhaps it's because she was told many times that she would fail as a child that she now has the sheer determination to succeed, or at least to try it. And she's well on her way, what was once a "little idea" is now in a start-up form. Because the technology is so basic, it can be implemented and used easily, but the impact it will have on people's lives and medical advancement in general is astounding.

> "I see force as a form of energy that it generates within ourselves. When times are tough or circumstances are difficult, force is what we need to get through."

It's impossible not to be inspired when hearing Sonia talk so passionately about nanotechnology, and her ability to make complex concepts so accessible has allowed her to share her ideas with tens of thousands of people on several platforms such Ted-X, Wired Health, and WEF. Imagining a nanometre as a billionth of a metre or understanding that each individual cell holds 2 metres of DNA is perhaps beyond normal comprehension, but Sonia's ability to capture imagination and spark curiosity goes a long way. Her unbounded passion for scientific research has now also extended to diagnosing life-threatening diseases, also after years of researching nanomaterials, Sonia is working on "a new generation of potential antibiotics that work in a completely different way to the ones we have now." Another game changer for a world that is fast becoming antibiotic resistant.

To find inspiration and intellectual stimulation, she likes to travel and surround herself with like-minded people. Beyond these incredible feats of scientific research, Sonia's personal aspirations are very simple, "I just want to be happy, when I'm happy, I'm creative, and innovative and that is the Sonia I like to be".

FORCE

I see force as a form of energy that it generates within ourselves. When times are tough or circumstances are difficult, force is what we need to get through. By being with my family, good friends and working, undoubtedly, is where I generate this energy. And according to my friends, sometimes can be contagious, which by the way, I love it!!!

STEVEN FOSTER

Founder and CEO - One Golden Nugget

The Believer

Steven has been instrumental in introducing me to self-reflection and expression. Our paths crossed at a mobility panel event, which I was moderating. Later, over coffee, he invited me to talk about myself, leading to a profound conversation where I shared thoughts I hadn't voiced before. Steven's impact on my life is undeniable. His unique ability to navigate through life's highs and lows is truly remarkable. It was in those moments with him that I truly understood that there is no such thing as failure.

Having run 11 marathons, 100 half marathons, and cycled almost 1000 miles along the length of Britain, creative entrepreneur Steven Foster could be considered an accomplished athlete. Like most sports competitors, he is only too aware that being an athlete is 70% mental and 30% physical. "You have a choice to create barriers of not being good enough, being too old, not having trained enough, not being fit enough." For Steven, training his body is really all about training his mind, and it's at the last hurdle of the 26 mile run that he relies on his mental strength to push him through to the finish line. "When you reach 20 or 21 miles, your body has just had enough, then it's a matter of controlling your mind."

Long distance running offers a convenient metaphor for Steven's career to date. He started his first business at the age of 19, replicating cassette tapes, within 5 years, he was duplicating 500,000 per month. He went on to create a student lifestyle website, build a record label that sold millions of copies, and own Dreamscape, one of the world's leading dance brands. But just like running a marathon, it's been a hard slog with a lot of barriers in the way. When most people would have thrown in the towel, Steven continued, always looking forward and breaking down those barriers.

Life is a Marathon, not a Sprint

As the founder of One Golden Nugget, a network of thought leaders sharing their treasures of wisdom, Steven has a few nuggets of his own. It may sound cliche to compare his career to a rollercoaster, but it has indeed been a series of ups and downs, which, ironically, puts him in the best position to advise others. "It's about having a sense of purpose, and not stopping - that's the only failure there is." He's also a man of many ideas, maybe too many to juggle, and has learned to be more focused on one thing at a time. "You have to train yourself as a creative entrepreneur to park ideas up, be laser focused on one thing, and get it done."

In an effort to share more nuggets of wisdom, life lessons, and business acumen, his bespoke publishing company, "One Golden Nugget" aims to shine a spotlight on some of the most interesting and influential individuals. With a unique ability to bring people from all walks of life together, Steven has inspired CEOs, founders, philanthropists, scientists, artists, activists, futurists, entrepreneurs, and freethinkers to share their wisdom, thoughts, ideas, and experiences with the world.

> ## "I truly believe that 99% of people want to do the best for other people."

Speaking at Gitex 2021 with Reebok Founder Joe Foster

Like many entrepreneurs, Steven has experienced both ends of the pendulum, incredible success and extreme financial hardship. Obviously, he acknowledges which state he prefers. However, now that he's matured and been able to reflect on what gives life meaning, he's less reliant on grandeur and accolades, recognizing instead that "beauty lies in the simplicity of things."

Working 9-5

Steven knew early on that a 9-5 job wasn't for him. Since he was 19, he has only worked for himself, preferring to risk failure doing what he loves rather than be stuck in a job he hates. This reluctance to buckle down and tow the line was influenced by his observations of his father, who felt he "sacrificed himself" in a job he hated to put food on the table. "It was painful to see. My father wanted to be a cartoonist, but he never had the strength to follow his dreams because he felt he had to buy things for his family." Steven admits that it takes an element of selfishness and a certain lack of fear. "I remember my early 30s, I had 2 kids, a wife, and a mortgage, and I still said, I'm not getting a job, I'll find a way - and I did".

He cautions against letting fear and complacency hold you back, suggesting instead that the key to life is to "dive in." It's better to take risks, and if there are mistakes, you learn from them and come out a better person. "You never go back to where you were previously because you have an awareness of it. You've gained knowledge and experience."

"Beauty lies in the simplicity of things."

Indeed, Steven did follow his dreams, taking big risks along the way. Sometimes they paid off, sometimes they didn't, but either way, he always persevered. At the age of 31, his hugely successful business collapsed overnight, causing him to fall into a deep depression. He lost all his money, but more importantly, he lost his identity. From owning one of the world's leading dance organisations to sweeping a factory floor, Steven's career path has taken him on an thrilling journey of highs and lows, gains and losses, to become a more circumspect man, a less materialistic man, and above all, a man who advocates "love in every interaction and thought."

"You never go back to where you were previously because you have an awareness of it. You've gained knowledge and experience."

All You Need is Love

Steven's difficult times are well documented, but he again takes comfort in the recognition that the difficult times have "arrived to teach you something." His wisdom is down to his One Golden Nugget, "I love people. I love talking with people. I love being with people. I love people more than anything else." It's clear where his priorities lie, and as a self-confessed people person, Steven savours the life lessons he's learned through his contacts at One Golden Nugget. The genuine and transparent conversations he has had with global leaders in business have taught him crucial lessons in self-reflection, optimism, and gratitude, something that's restored his confidence in the future of humanity.

His approach to life is also very influenced by the 1960s philosophy of togetherness. Imagining a world 50 years from now, he hopes that society will have broken free from harmful and limiting stereotypes, instead viewing each other as complex individuals and, more importantly, human beings. Considering the Beatles' song, *All You Need Is Love* an enduring "message to the world", he's firmly committed to placing people before profit, and responding to hate with compassion.

> "I love people. I love talking with people. I love being with people. I love people more than anything else."

SUBHRA DAS

Founder and CEO - Aladdin.life

The Challenger

I had always known Subhra in a corporate context. He was my client based out of Saudi, leading the launch of a new Telecom operator. But recently, our conversations have unveiled a far more spiritual side of him. He spoke about the varied manifestations of 'force' – from the spirit that transcends time and space to the life-sustaining chi or prana, symbolizing our vital breath. He described the soul, or atma, as the essence that animates our physical being. Subhra emphasized our consciousness as both a silent observer and witness, highlighting a deeper understanding of our existence. Properties of omniscience, omnipotence and omnipresence.

Subhra Das is the founder and CEO of Aladdin, a start-up that is addressing the biggest customer experience gap in the telecom industry by building a global marketplace for mobile and broadband services. Subhra is a former senior telecom executive, having done CEO and multiple CMO roles with top telecom companies around the world, including 6 successful telecom start-ups. He has lived and worked in 12 countries across Europe, India, Middle East and Africa, with companies like du, STC, Ooredoo, Orange, Vodafone, Glo, Hexacom (now Airtel) and Lebara Mobile Europe.

An engineer by training, Subhra is an alumnus of Harvard Business School (AMP) and the Indian Institute of Management, Ahmedabad (MBA). He is an avid guitar player in several styles and holds a Masters Certificate in guitar from Berklee College of Music (Online). Holistic health, meditation, yoga, ancient wisdom traditions, quantum physics, and the convergence of science and spirituality are his other areas of keen interest.

The Relentless Pursuit of Purpose

Subhra's journey into entrepreneurship was seamless after a successful corporate career in the telecom world. "We live in unprecedented times with several paradigm shifts. This is an age of disruptive technologies and business models, with the promise to make human lives exponentially better. There is also the quest for finding the deeper meaning and true purpose in our lives, and a growing recognition and faith in our infinite potential. These have all inspired me to follow my own dreams.'

Subhra is obsessed with innovation and has left behind a trail of pioneering work in the telecom world. Most of the telecom start-ups where he worked in leadership roles are today multi-billion dollar companies. He also conceived, created and launched one of the world's first digital mobile operators for STC in KSA- a model that has been replicated by Telecom operators worldwide.

Aladdin was created with the purpose of addressing some of the greatest challenges facing mobile service users and telecom operators. Telecom networks are the gateway to the digital economy. However, as data usage is growing exponentially and customer spending is not, the sustainability of regular investments in telecom networks is under threat.

"Entrepreneurs are driven by purpose while being comfortable with uncertainty and the unknown. Ultimately, it is about self-discovery, creation and tenacity".

"Ai and decentralised technologies like blockchain will reshape our world, and blockchain will ensure a more equitable distribution of wealth." As a musician, Subhra sees the need for helping music artists achieve financial security. "Musicians contribute significantly but only a few make it big. The majority of musicians have to struggle financially. Technological advances have helped fans and record labels, but not the musicians", he adds.

Subhra underscores the importance of five key factors for a successful entrepreneurial journey. The first is about purpose, vision and faith. "Purpose not only gives you a sense of fulfilment, but keeps you steadfast in your commitment in times of uncertainty. Vision guides, inspires and attracts the end state. Faith moves mountains." Secondly, support from family and friends, particularly in the early stages, is very key. Third, building a great team. "You're only as good as your team. The team needs to be inspired and connected to your story to unleash their full potential." Fourth, it is all about story-telling and execution. And finally, entrepreneurship is about tenacity and realising that you fail only when you give up. Every failure can be a pivot towards a better idea and bigger success.

Finding Our Infinite Potential: The Real You

Subhra is driven by the realisation that we all have unlimited potential, and are limited only by our imagination. All possibilities exist and can be manifested through our thoughts, emotions and actions, including programming your sub-conscious mind. It is now commonly understood that

"Purpose not only gives you a sense of fulfilment, but keeps you steadfast in your commitment in times of uncertainty."

everything around us is about energy, and that we create our realities through vibrations and their frequencies.

Subhra is drawn to metaphysical themes like the meaning of existence and reality, the nature of time and space, and the hard problem of science-consciousness. "Some ancient wisdom traditions refer to consciousness as the real and unlimited you. This real you exist beyond the labels and the identities we carry - father, son, CEO etc. Behind our physical senses, lies our mind and behind the mind is the real you – as a witness and as pure consciousness." Consciousness supposedly has three properties: omniscience (all knowing) omnipotence (can do anything) and omnipresence (being anywhere). "To access this realm, you have to go beyond the mind, for which calming and quieting the mind are essential through practices like meditation and chanting.'

"I want to share a great quote I came across in a Times magazine article on Carlos Santana back in the mid-nineties. Santana quoted a profound line in the article and described how this line made a lasting impact on his music and his evolution. It was from his spiritual guru Sri Chinmoy: 'To find yourself, you have to lose yourself first'." This beautiful quote has helped me immensely since then. And hope it helps you too on your journey to find and unleash your true potential.

"You're only as good as your team. The team
needs to be inspired and connected to your
story to unleash their full potential."

XAVI ANGLADA

Managing Director - Accenture GLC

The World Citizen

Xavi is a man of many missions. He sees Force as the unrelenting drive to better our world. Having come from humble beginnings, he has always had a growth mindset, and has used it to push small ideas and teams to become global, transformative and always purpose-driven. He channels his energy into creating opportunities for others to thrive and achieve. He believes in the power of human potential, innovation and fostering an environment where dreams don't just live, but flourish. Having spoken to Xavi and meeting his beautiful family, it's clear that he's committed to using his growth and learnings to make a positive impact on the lives of many.

Xavi Anglada is one of the few people who can truly regard himself as a "world citizen." Having lived in four different continents; Europe, Africa, Asia, and North America, he has worked as a global consultant in more than 40 countries. Although now based in Dubai, he has become a globetrotter, and is always thinking about what is coming next. "I'm never in a place to say I'm here forever, I'm here because I'm contributing towards something, but I don't know where I'm going tomorrow."

He confesses that the "purpose and impact" he was initially aiming for was materialistic, perhaps due to where he started in life. However, now that he has

"What I know is what I've learned, not from books but from people, and that has shaped me."

achieved wealth and success, he's looking to "give back". Although he hasn't yet worked out how he is going to achieve this, he does know that he wants to teach in universities and schools around the globe. Public speaking is a passion for Xavi, "because it allows me to talk about topics and also learn from other people that know a lot more than me."

Xavi has had two great influences in his life, his mother and maternal grandfather. His mother owned a small bakery, and he explains that "we had a very humble start. I owned just one pair of clothes and a pair of sandals." As an 8-year-old, he worked in the bakery, starting at the bottom cleaning dishes, then at 11 he started baking cakes, and at 13, he started selling the cakes, which is when his entrepreneurial spirit kicked in. At such a young age, Xavi already saw the value in making products and selling them, and he constantly tried to improve his cakes by customising them for his customers. Above all, he developed essential social skills, communication skills, and empathy. The experience shaped him into what he is today; a great communicator with a growth mindset.

Whilst his peers were playing, Xavi was usually working, so he grew up without a friendship group. His mother became a "very, very big influence" on him, which he didn't appreciate at the time, but as he got older, he learned to cherish the impact she had on him. Decades later, she was to prove an essential part in his decision to move to Dubai, when she encouraged him to take a risk and grab the opportunity that was being offered to him.

Xavi worked at the bakery until he left to study telecom engineering at Ramon Llull University in Barcelona, and it was there that he began to flourish and develop new and lasting friendships. He stopped looking at what he didn't have and focused more on what he did have, "becoming more self-conscious and self-convinced." In other words, Xavi started to believe in himself. He got a part-time job at the university and started developing his interest in becoming a teacher.

"Be daring, and take risks."

A Professional Dilemma

Xavi was given a choice between two very different pathways when he was offered both a PhD placement at the university, and also a job at Hewlett Packard (HP). It was a choice that would define his future life and career. He already knew a senior manager at HP from his hometown, and he was the one to sway Xavi's decision to join the company rather than pursuing the academic path. Their relationship has stood the test of time, with his mentor eventually becoming his mentee. The two men have gone on a long journey together, and there is still more to come, "we constantly meet and walk together and brainstorm around life and work matters, we call it the Power Walk."

Xavi made the right decision at the right time, he had a mentor who listened and gave him constant advice and support, he was able to travel, and he was provided the opportunity to explore, "be daring, and take risks." Clearly, the experiences and relationships Xavi met at HP prepared him well for future leadership roles. During the 1990s, all production in Europe was being relocated to Asia, and Xavi was provided the opportunity to travel there and "learn from the suppliers to bring the procurement and manufacturing to Asia."

At the time, it was a valuable experience and one that he is still grateful for, but in time Xavi outgrew the company, and after taking his MBA, he left HP and went to work for a small strategy consulting firm, later acquired by what is today Oliver Wyman. "Keeping

> "I need to be close to people who inspire me because then I can inspire others."

close to visionaries is important to me, I need to be close to people who inspire me because then I can inspire others." This career stage took him to work across Europe, North and South Africa and the Middle East. "I liked the projects I had in Algeria and South Africa because there was a human part to them. Visiting the people who had little shops, selling phone SIMs or groceries, and looking at distribution, it was very different from the sophisticated way things were done in Europe." This experience also widened his exposure to senior leadership behaviours and gave him a passion for Africa, where he later went on to live for "the best three years of [his] life."

From Spain to Dubai

Getting married and starting a family meant Xavi needed to be a little more settled, and so he took a new position in Spain, working for the "challenger for Telefonica." After two years and some ups and downs, he became partner and COO for Delta Partners, based in Dubai. It was a risk to leave a stable job with an established company, but Xavi is a risk-taker and someone who was continually looking for the next adventure. With the encouragement of his mother,

who told him to "never miss a single opportunity", he packed up and moved to Dubai.

For Xavi, Dubai has been a place where his family has grown and flourished. He has a diverse group of friends from different industries, backgrounds, and countries and his children are part of a multicultural community, "beyond what I was building, the family was growing in a way that I would never have dreamed of before." It's been a risk that has paid off for Xavi both personally and professionally, he has a number of startups that his wife is involved with, keeping their minds always fresh and hungry. He confirms, "it's been a great journey for the whole family."

Xavi comes across as a devoted lifelong learner, and he admits that it is conversations with his children who make him re-evaluate his perspective the most, "they have developed a wonderful critical thinking process that made me think about my view on stereotypes. When I listen to how they approach their problems or talk about how they would like to learn, work, or have the stability they want in life, it's super interesting."

The Next Thing

After helping scale Delta Partners, he was ready for the next thing and took a role as CEO of Cash Credit, a FinTech, non-banking financial institution, aiming to bring economic inclusion to "very disfavoured countries", like the Philippines, South Africa, and Cameroon. By creating "very tech-driven decision algorithms", the company was able to provide microloans to small businesses, helping them to expand and thrive.

Xavi then moved to Accenture, which gave him the opportunity to lead the digital transformation of large public and private corporations. "I really loved every moment of the process, especially recruiting people very different from myself, with very different minds, and we achieved great things." One of his proudest accomplishments was the involvement in delivering Expo 2020 Dubai in the United Arab Emirates, which was "an amazing contribution to bringing the vision of this country to reality."

Whilst a very successful businessman, Xavi is an entrepreneur at heart and his greatest passion is building things from scratch. Moving from telecom to fintech and then to mega companies like Accenture has satisfied his entrepreneurial spirit in the way he could be part of a company but still "explore the unknown, learn from scratch, and be inspired." Although he has not yet "planned what's next", he does know what he wants from his next big venture, and that's a sense of purpose. "I have yet to find my biggest purpose, and so I am searching for my next thing."

That next thing could be his latest start-up endeavour, focusing on health technology. After losing his father to cancer, finding tech that can diagnose the disease early is a personal project for Xavi. Together with the Head of the Nanotechnology Department at Oxford University, Xavi's latest start-up business is focusing on early diagnostics of diseases, such as childhood leukaemia. "This is the type of place where I want to spend time and put my money to work." He expresses that his focus is not making money but making an impact, and the start-up has already patented its nanotechnology for diagnostics.

The 'next thing' for Xavi isn't just focused on work, however. He's a man of many passions, an avid reader of all genres, a lover of classical music and one day he'd love to have the time to learn the piano. Using technology for good is also a major focus for him, and he believes that with its proper utilisation, humans can fast track the implementation of the sustainable development goals adopted by the UN. He loves to travel to universities, sharing his knowledge and wisdom with younger generations, and he wants to "educate people about leveraging technology to change big problems that can save the lives of millions – this is where I want to put my money to work." With more entrepreneurs and business leaders searching for a purpose beyond the materialistic, and adopting the same philanthropic attitude as Xavi, perhaps there will be a positive future ahead for the world.

"Never miss a
single opportunity."

ELENI KITRA

Founder and CEO, KITRA Inclusive

ex-Meta, Omnicom, Sony, Top100 Asia's Women Power Leaders 2023

Life is like a bullet train

My life often feels like a whirlwind comparable to a speeding bullet train, constantly moving without a pause. When I reflect on my journey, I think about the defining moments that shaped who I am and my path to success. Growing up in Greece, I was always more clear about what I didn't desire than what I did. Caught between wanting a stable, familiar life and craving a career filled with global travel and fresh experiences, I navigated a world where my interactions were local, and my only window to the outside world was through media.

"The power of reflection
I don't grow old, I grow powerful."

As a child, I always wanted to be a gymnast, but I lacked the necessary resources and role models to pursue it as a career. Either way, it's intriguing how this curiosity and desire to explore led me to the business world. Now, I embrace my identity as a 'Woman of Many Missions,' always eager to embark on new ventures and experiences.

As a child, I always acted instinctively, embracing a wide range of experiences that have shaped my journey so far. During my time at university, I was eager to explore and grow. I balanced a variety of jobs, from babysitting to night shifts at the State Mail Company, with my love for creative and athletic endeavors. Whether it was playing in a band, despite my admittedly average singing, participating in archery and shooting, or engaging in arts like painting, knitting, and jewelry making, each experience was a part of my journey of self-discovery and experimentation.

Right after my studies I moved into the corporate world. And from that time I spent almost 30 years in building and growing business across the world and in diverse industries. I have been blessed to work for some of the most outstanding companies, meet some of the most inspiring people, travel around the world, and become open-minded and open-hearted. My first big career moment was when I joined Sony and after a few years of working in various roles, I took on the Sales and Marketing role for PlayStation. I had never played video games before in my entire life, but I found it thrilling to be part of the launch of one of the biggest disruptions in the gaming industry ever and making it the market leader. We successfully shifted the gamer demographic, transforming PlayStation into the ultimate entertainment device. I still remember the endless days I was playing PlayStation games with my husband and friends. One of the most memorable moments was when I was trying to put Playstation booths in the chill out rooms in night clubs, and everyone thought I was crazy to try something like that. The idea was finally a huge success. During my time at Sony I also developed some incredibly strongest friendships, ones that I still value to this day.

Post-Sony, I transitioned to Multichoice, a South African firm, where I built up and led the Pay TV Advertising Business's commercial team. After a fruitful two-year tenure there, I progressed to the next significant chapter in my career journey. In 1999, I embarked on a new venture with Tempo OMD (Omnicom Group) in Greece, where I established their Digital Business. Over the following 12 years, my team and I propelled Omnicom to the forefront of the market, maintaining our leadership position for 12 consecutive years. This period was marked by numerous awards, the acquisition of new clients, and the creation of successful campaigns. This achievement was due to the steadfast commitment of an exceptional team, marked by countless hours of hard work and dedication.

Both professionally and personally, this era was incredibly rewarding and productive.
In those transformative years, I journeyed into motherhood, welcoming my first child in 2000 and my second in 2003. Reflecting on that period, I recognize the complexities of melding motherhood with a career. More than the external challenges, it was the internal struggle, the absence of role models in a world still bound by stereotypes about women's roles, that was most daunting. My resilience and a 'no victim' mindset were crucial, as was the unwavering support of my husband, who was my pillar. This experience deepened my conviction; given the choice between a supportive partner and a great job, the former is irreplaceable, while the latter can always be found anew.

My Transformation

My husband and I always wanted to work abroad, yet aligning our careers seemed almost impossible. In 2012, everything changed when he received an offer to move to Dubai, and I embraced the opportunity without hesitation, despite the emotional challenge of leaving behind family, friends, colleagues and a career. Now, after 12 years in Dubai, I can reflect on how profoundly transformative this journey has been for me and my family. Starting afresh – establishing a home, social connections, and career – was daunting yet exhilarating.

Barely six months into my new life in Dubai, I embarked on an exhilarating journey with Facebook, and it is now I realize how pivotal that time was. I joined a small, yet ambitious team, charged with the task of broadening our advertising reach across the Middle East and Africa. This role was more than a career progression; it was a journey of personal and professional growth. Reflecting on my nearly decade-long tenure at Meta (ex Facebook), it wasn't just about the varied global business roles I undertook, or the great results we implemented, and the world-class best practices we delivered. It was the privilege of working with and leading global teams. It was about the incredible individuals I met along the way. These relationships evolved into deep friendships and mentorships, enriching my life far beyond the professional realm. This experience was transformative, extending beyond professional accomplishments to enduring relationships that have enriched my life profoundly.

I have always been a champion and outspoken ambassador for equality, particularly gender equality. But in the past 10 years, I have really found my purpose advocating for equity in the workplace, ensuring everyone has a fair chance at opportunities and resources. During my tenure at Facebook, I had the opportunity to work at a regional and global scale with the Leadership, the Diversity-Equity and Inclusion (DEI) and Human Resources teams, the powerful Employees Resources Groups (ERGs), and we collectively created one of the strongest and authentic organizational culture. I have collaborated with numerous organizations and inspirational leaders worldwide, dedicating my efforts to advancing gender equity both regionally and globally. My role has been pivotal in leading and advocating for women in leadership positions globally.

We all know that when people come first, businesses thrive. My goal has always been to empower people and organizations to be the catalyst for growth and success by fostering a diverse and inclusive workplace.

AB

I Am Not One Thing

In 2017, I organized our Facebook Women leadership meeting, and we had an enlightening workshop, dedicated to crafting a clear vision-mission for our women's resource group. This workshop was a revelation. I realized that we should not be defined by a single trait or skill; we are extraordinarily multifaceted, blending diverse capabilities and cross-pollinating strengths to create multi-talented personas.

This realization sparked a desire in me to showcase the value of being more than just one thing. I was inspired to write this book celebrating the amazing people I've encountered in my journey, highlighting their rich layers of personality. This book is a tribute to those remarkable individuals who strive for a better world, embodying the essence of being a force for positive change. It narrates the stories of transformative leaders worldwide who are making a significant impact in various fields, fostering a more dynamic, inclusive, and sustainable world.

My journey as a mother has been the most significant experience, filled with life's joys and complexities. My daughter once humorously remarked that if I didn't work, I'd be miserable and challenging to live with. This light-hearted comment holds a profound truth about balancing parenting and professional life. I've learned there's no perfect work-life balance; it's more about juggling various responsibilities – some like delicate glass, others like resilient plastic. There have been moments of forgetfulness and near misses, not prideful but human. Today, my family serves as my personal 'Wise Advisory Board,' offering candid, invaluable insights. They've become my greatest motivators, fueling my personal and professional growth. I've always believed in the importance of choosing a supportive partner over just a good job because a partner significantly shapes our life's journey. In 1997, facing a career opportunity and the thought of starting a family, my husband encouraged me to take the job, reminding me that there's always time for family later.

This decision led to more significant opportunities and a seat on the Board of Directors. Above all, I've learned the importance of cherishing moments with family and friends, ensuring to always enhance my life with laughter and joy.

Breaking the Mold: My Leap from Corporate Life to Entrepreneurship

In the Summer of 2020, while I was on vacation with my family in Greece, I first expressed my desire to start my own business. At the time, I was still hesitant but a year later, I had left 30 years of corporate experience behind to establish KITRA Inclusive, an Inclusive Leadership consulting company. The transition from my corporate career to entrepreneurship was a daring jump into new, unexplored realms, filled with both challenges and exhilaration. However, the invaluable insights gained from corporate experience greatly helped in establishing my new venture. Nevertheless, my entrepreneurial journey has been a path of self-discovery, unveiling aspects of myself that I had never encountered before. It's a dynamic blend of leveraging past learnings while continuously evolving and growing in unexpected ways. I fully embraced what I call my '4 C's: Curiosity, Collaboration, Courage, and Commitment,' which guided my journey. Curiosity opened my eyes to new possibilities, and collaboration brought diverse minds together, creating a synergy where the whole was greater than the sum of its parts. This journey was a leap into the unknown, filled with learning and excitement.

Fear Not

Aristotle's perspective on leadership — creating an environment where potential can flourish — deeply resonates with me. My journey, marked by a desire for diverse experiences, was about learning to harness the power of my inner voice. I embraced a 'fear not' attitude, motivated to learn, take risks, commit, and deliver. This drive, coupled with a commitment to leading a purposeful and fulfilling life, transformed challenges into opportunities for growth, teaching me the invaluable lesson of leading fearlessly and authentically.

Women@
LEADERSHIP DAY
"I am not just one thing"
Please take your women
badge and choose anot
BLIND OR

Author Bio

Eleni is a global leader in business management, digital transformation, communication, and marketing, with over three decades of experience leading international companies in multiple industries and geographies. She is the Founder and CEO of KITRA Inclusive, an inclusive leadership consulting firm.

She previously held the position of Regional Head of Automotive and Mobility at Facebook. Her career also includes roles as Managing Director at OMD Digital of Omnicom Media Group, and Commercial Director at Multichoice, a prominent entertainment firm. Additionally, she played a key role in the team that spearheaded the launch of PlayStation in Europe.

As a global leader in supporting women in tech, Eleni has spearheaded women in leadership for Facebook EMEA and Global, founded the Women in Mobility GCC Forum, and is a passionate mentor and gender equality ambassador.

Her influence extends to the MENA business community, where she mentors startups and co-chairs the Business Innovator Committee at Dubai Capital Club. She also serves as the Executive Director of the Advertising Business Group.

Eleni lectures on leadership and entrepreneurship and she is chairing the Middlesex Innovation Hub. Recognized as one of the Top 100 Asia's Women Power Leaders and a CIOTimes Influential Woman to Watch in 2023, Eleni is advocating for innovation, inclusivity, and sustainability in business and beyond.

182

DO YOU HAVE A STORY TO TELL?
WWW.ONEGOLDENNUGGET.COM